The Sensible Girl's Guide to Emigrating Elegantly

The Sensible Girl's Guide to Emigrating Elegantly

Elegant Escapology Made Easy

Sally Corner

with illustrations by the author

First published in Great Britain 2010

A & C Black Publishers Ltd
36 Soho Square, London W1D 3QY
www.acblack.com

A CIP record for this book is available from the British Library.

ISBN: 9–781–4081–2175–7

This book is produced using paper that is made from wood grown in
managed, sustainable forests. It is natural, renewable and recyclable. The
logging and manufacturing processes conform to the environmental
regulations of the country of origin.

Design by Fiona Pike, Pike Design, Winchester
Typeset by Saxon Graphics, Derby
Printed and bound in Great Britain by Cox & Wyman, Reading, RG1 8EX

To my husband.

'More than the ocean.'

CONTENTS

The Beginning Bit   **Once Upon a Time...**   xii
My emigrating story – leaving the UK

Introduction   **Just What is This Little Book for Exactly?**   xxi
Can a book really help you emigrate?

Chapter 1   **Are You Sure You Want to Emigrate?**   1
Facts and figures that explore the emigration
phenomenon and help you decide whether or
not you really want to emigrate

Chapter 2   **What's Your 'Sensible Status'?**   16
Single, dating, married, kids, retired...can
anyone emigrate?

Chapter 3   **Getting Started**   38
Finding your goals and writing your Wish List
The Top Ten Emigration Destinations for
Sensible British Girls

Chapter 4   **Narrowing Down Your Search**   52
Finding that special place to live in Your New
Country

Chapter 5   **The Master Plan**   62
Getting your emigrating equipment together
and getting organised

| Chapter 6 | **The Paperwork** | 74 |
| | Looking into the legalities of entering Your New Country | |

Chapter 7	**Planting Seeds (future planning)**	93
	Finding the cash	95
	Finding a home	96
	Finding a job	99
	Finding a friend	104
	Finding the fun	107

Chapter 8	**Tying Up Loose Ends (past management)**	109
	Tying up your finances	111
	Tying up your property	118
	Tying up your job	123
	Tying up your car	125
	Tying up your pet	128
	Tying up your health	132
	Tying up your stuff (and storing or shipping it)	134

| Chapter 9 | **Leaving Loved Ones** | 148 |
| | How to say goodbye and host a divine departing do! | |

| Chapter 10 | **Travel Arrangements** | 157 |
| | Helpful hints on booking flights, insurance and accommodation | |

| Chapter 11 | **Fourteen Days and Counting...** | 165 |
| | Practical and not-so-practical checklists of 'things to do' | |

Chapter 12   **Pre-emigrating Ailments**   176
Emotional troubleshooting before you leave
the UK

Chapter 14*   **Packing**   186
What to pack and how to pack it

Chapter 15   **Twenty-four Hours and Counting...**   196
Your last few hours in the UK...and what to
do with them

Chapter 16   **Airport Departure Technique**   201
How to leave the UK elegantly

The Middle Bit   **...In a Land Far, Far Away...**   206
My emigrating story – arriving in My New
Country

    The Sensible Girl's In-flight Quiz   214
Find out whether how elegant your emigration
has been so far

Chapter 17   **Airport Arrival Technique**   225
How to arrive in Your New Country elegantly

Chapter 18   **Settling In**   228
Emigration tools   228
Paperwork and finance   231–232
Renting   233
Employment   238

---

*   Sensible = Superstitious...so stop looking for Chapter 13.

Contents

	Social life	243
	Getting around	248
	Media	249
	Wildlife	251
	Culture	252

Chapter 19   **Homesickness**   256
Understanding it, coping with it and getting
rid of it

Chapter 20   **The Perks: Reasons to Be Cheerful**   274
Ten reminders of why it's great that you've
emigrated

Chapter 21   **Post-emigrating Ailments**   281
Emotional troubleshooting when you arrive in
your new country

Chapter 22   **Your Emigration De-brief**   299
How do you feel?

The End Bit   **...Happily Ever After?**   303
My emigrating story – how did it all work out?

Acknowledgements   311

Index   323

PREFACE

sensible *adj.* having or showing good sense.

emigrate *v.* to leave one country to go to settle in another.

elegantly *adv.* **elegant** *adj.* tasteful, refined, and dignified in appearance or style.[1]

THE BEGINNING BIT

ONCE UPON A TIME...

...In a not so distant land just down the road from the M4, a little urban princess named Sally grew up with her loving parents, King John and Queen Carolyn, in the beautiful Kingdom of Acton Town. She was blessed with all the things that Inner London princesses are usually blessed with: nice little friends to play with, a pet hamster and a shiny new pair of rollerboots.

As the years went by, the little princess was taken by her beloved parents to exotic holiday destinations such as Worthing, Skegness and Filey Brigg where she enjoyed playing on England's golden shores, feeling the sand between her frostbitten toes and splashing around in the icy waters. Her childhood was both wonderful and average at the same time.

When Princess Sally grew to be a petulant teenager, King John and Queen Carolyn decided that their daughter's horizons needed broadening and so they decreed that it was time to take her on a magical holiday to foreign shores on the other side of the world. So, with royal trunks packed, travelling arrangements finalised and plant-watering instructions left with the neighbours, the princess and her parents left for the Great Red Continent.

The princess was in heaven. Aside from the rare and intriguing sight of blue sky and a bright ball of light that people called 'the sun', there were unusual beasts that bounced and monsters with big, sharp teeth lurking in the depths of the turquoise ocean. There were serpents that could kill with a single sneeze and spiders the size of dinner tables. The natives all had smiles on their faces, drank icy cold jugs of ale and ate pies. The beaches were warm enough for the young princess to remove her wool-lined thermal undergarments and don a most unusual outfit made from string and triangles. The young princess felt happy and secretly planned to revisit the Great Red Continent when she grew up.

After a long journey back to the Kingdom of Acton Town, Princess Sally knuckled down to revising for exams, scribing love letters to her sweet Norwegian pop-prince, Morten Harket, watching the chronicles of Ramsay Street on her very own television set and began the arduous task of growing up.

Time passed. Boy bands separated and fashions got less shoulder-paddy but the princess never forgot that Great Red Continent. When the princess became a young woman fresh out of film college, she decided she was going to direct films for a couple of years, before she got a proper job. However, the cruel beast that calls itself the film industry proved a tad challenging so, instead, she worked for a gentleman called Mr W H Smith, selling birthday cards and paper clips. It was a busy store and she was a busy girl, but alas, she was not a happy girl and the King and Queen knew this. She felt that there must be more to life than living in the Kingdom of Acton Town with her parents, selling stationery...and then she remembered her beloved Red Continent.

The princess had heard on the royal grapevine that fellow princesses from neighbouring kingdoms were no longer following the traditional career route of getting a job, working their tiny posteriors off, meeting a prince, having sixteen children and then living happily ever after. No, these fair maidens were abandoning their lives for approximately one year and going on wild adventures around the world, commonly known as an Annus Gapus.

Upon learning this, Princess Sally decided that she wanted a piece of the action and announced to her parents that she was going to go on a voyage of personal discovery, back to the Red Continent. She was unyielding in her manner and passionate in her quest to arrange her Annus Gapus and she could not be persuaded against such a voyage. And so it was decreed that the princess would travel, with a pack on her back, and learn the ways of the world.

Princess Sally travelled far and wide across the Great Red Continent. She jumped from tall bridges with elasticated rope tied to her ankles. She swam with the tropical fish on the rainbow reefs and drank copious amounts of wine, thanks to a bloke called Jacob who owned a creek. She even learnt how to unwrap a Crunchie bar wedged in a man's crotch...without using her hands. Not the classiest of Backpackers' Drinking Games, granted, but what the hell, she was learning the ways of the world...and she was having a great time!

Time flew by and the Red Continent's bureaucratic scribes decreed that the princess's time was up and that she must leave for Blighty post-haste. So, with a heavy heart and a discreet piercing, she returned home once more.

She felt different, she felt alive, she felt invincible, but the grey, dowdy subjects in the Kingdom of Acton Town did not seem to notice. For they were too busy kicking each other out of the way to get the disabled seat on the District line. And so a cloud descended over the sad princess.

MIND THE GAP

Over the years, Princess Sally had a modest number of suitors who tried to woo her. Some were wretched, some broke her heart and some ever so slightly bored her. Once she even met a handsome chap who wanted to whisk her away to Africa and study lions! But things never quite worked out with these gentlemen. Time ticked on...and the cloud remained hanging over the princess's head and there seemed nothing she or the rest of the court could do to remove it.

In desperation the princess left the Kingdom of Acton Town and moved into a rather fabulous Chelsea gaff with a nice nobleman named Sir Fairway who worked in IT. She landed herself a plum job with a top film publicity company and got to hang out with film stars (and make their tea). She was living the high life – or so it seemed. But whatever she did and whoever she did it with she could not shake the golden shores of the Great Red Continent from her consciousness. And so the cloud remained.

She spoke to a soothsayer whose noble runes and badger's innards suggested that maybe she needed to change a few things, so she gave Sir Fairway the flick. But that didn't help.

Another year went by and the newly single Princess Sally was beginning to realise that the key to her happiness did not lie in some handsome prince's breeches but on the other side of the globe. So she began to plot and plan. She needed to escape the Kingdom of Acton Town once and for all...but this time it would be for good.

Then, one day, in the middle of all her plotting and planning, she received a 'ye maile'. It was from the Lion Boy (otherwise known as Lord Grenville). He'd decided not to go on permanent safari to deepest, darkest Africa and had become an accountant based in Olde Oxford Streete instead, just a few hundred yards up the road from Princess Sally's place of work. What a coincidence. He also explained that he'd been thinking of emigrating to the Red Continent and wondered if the princess, given her fascination with the place, knew how to go about it.

Princess Sally fainted.

When she recovered, they met and went for a few ales at a local tavern, to discuss their love of The Great Upside Down Land. Lord Grenville was handsomer than Princess Sally had remembered and devilishly funny to boot. As the evening drew to an end, the loud twang of a bow could be heard resonating from the depths of the Dog and Donkey and Cupid made a hasty exit out of the privy window.

Lord Grenville and Princess Sally moved quickly, for they now knew what they wanted. They employed the finest emigration experts to enhance their chances of being granted the right to live and work in the Great Red Continent. While doing so they spent the remains of their free time falling in love, selling Lord Grenville's house, quitting their jobs, saying farewell to family and friends, getting engaged and trying to avoid completely freaking out. It was a most busy, exciting and stressful time. But the prospect of going to live in their dream country Down Under was all they needed to keep them going. And so they waited for the Great Red Continent's bureaucratic scribes to grant them their residency.

And they waited...

and waited...

and waited...

and they got a bit bored of waiting and decided to go anyway.

So they placed everything in storage, waved goodbye to their loved ones and boarded the big bird that would fly them to their magical land far, far away.

Without the wax sealed residency papers they were not allowed to work (shame!) and so they purchased a trusty campervan. They decided that if they were going to live in this vast continent, they would need to know which kingdom would be best to settle in.

And so they drove...

and drove...

and argued a bit...

and drove...

and wondered if they'd made the right decision ...

and drove...

and sent some postcards...

and drove...

After driving around the entire circumference of the continent, having swam with friendly sharks, stared in awe at leaping crocodiles and swatted more flies than you could possibly imagine, the wax sealed residency papers had *still* not been granted. So, with heavy hearts, Princess Sally and Lord Grenville decided that they would have to return to their old lives.

And so they did.

They went back to their respective old jobs, moved back into their old neighbourhood, back to their local tavern and back to the same life they had left behind. And they were thoroughly depressed, for nothing had changed and everything was cold and grey.

Then, one chilly day in January a letter landed on their doorstep and it had a red wax seal on it. Princess Sally trod on it as she stumbled through the front door. She'd had yet another stressful day at the office dealing with crazy mental film stars and was in no mood for anything other than a large goblet of Chardonnay. Upon noticing the sealed envelope stuck to her shoe, she peeled it off and opened it with trembling hands...and fainted.

One month passed.

The princess and Lord Grenville stood in the Ye Throwe flight departure lounge, bidding soggy farewells to their families. And amongst all the crying, purchasing of glossy magazines and scouting around duty free for the latest Chanel nail polish, Princess Sally smiled to herself. For she was finally embarking on the adventure she'd always dreamt of...she was emigrating to Australia.

~~THE END~~

THE BEGINNING...

INTRODUCTION

JUST WHAT IS THIS BOOK FOR EXACTLY?

So now you know how my emigrating fairy tale began. How will yours go?

If you're reading this book, you must have had similar dreams of moving to a new and magical land, far, far away. You must also be teetering on the edge of the proverbial precipice, deciding whether to jump or not and wondering if you really can do it.

As you can tell from the previous pages, it took me ages to 'jump'. I started toying with the notion of living abroad in my early teens. I decided I wanted to emigrate to Australia in my mid-twenties. And I finally pulled my finger out and actually did something about it in my early thirties. That's a lot of faffing.

Now that I have emigrated, I have only one regret – that I didn't do it sooner. Especially as the main reason for delaying all those years wasn't because of money, or paperwork, or even leaving loved ones behind; it was simple, good old-fashioned lack of confidence.

When I started this book, I wasn't interested in writing one of those devilishly helpful 'moving abroad' guides. Those books provide a wealth of useful information and become an invaluable aid to emigrating, but they will not make a jot of difference to your life if you don't have the confidence to actually put them to use and emigrate. This is a rather obvious point, I know, but one that is all too often overlooked.

These days, most of us have the Internet at our fingertips. This can provide us with pretty much all the practical information we need, just as long as we have a rough idea of what we're looking for. However, what we are often in short supply of is a good helping of self-assurance and the belief that we really can *do* it. We need more than a catalogue of facts and figures to get us on the plane. We need encouragement, guidance and a friendly but firm shove in the right direction.

The world is getting smaller and the number of people who want to experience life in a different country is getting bigger. It's as simple as that. You only have to turn on the TV, read a bestseller or watch a film to realise that we all dream of escaping, every now and then.

Whether you are thinking of moving to New York or Nice, a small desert island on the Pacific Rim or indeed to the Great Red Continent itself, this book cannot tell you exactly how to do it – in fact, *no* book can. But it can give you an idea of what you need to be thinking about, help you deal with what you are worrying about and point out what you should be getting very, very excited about.

I want to give as much encouragement as possible to anyone who has had even a glimmer of an idea about moving abroad. For it is dreams like the ones you have while peering out of the bus on a rainy day in January that can turn into reality. So, although this book offers sensible, practical advice on emigrating elegantly, it is far more concerned with assuring you that you undoubtedly, most definitely, absolutely *can* do it!

From now on we will refer to the country to which you plan on emigrating to as Your New Country (YNC). So please remember this, as I am in no way suggesting, in a somewhat dyslexic manner, that everybody should emigrate to New York City.

One final reason for writing this book is to strongly urge all my nearest and dearest friends and family to emigrate as well. Being a Sensible Girl who now lives in sunny Australia, I have now reached stage two of my Master Plan – to persuade everyone else to have a go.

So come on, what are you waiting for?

CHAPTER I

ARE YOU SURE YOU WANT TO EMIGRATE?

Never go abroad. It's a dreadful place.
EARL OF CARDIGAN[1]

I want you to do a little experiment. Ask the next person you talk to whether they know anyone who has emigrated, anyone who is planning on emigrating or anyone who has ever tinkered with the notion of emigrating. I can pretty much guarantee that everyone you talk to will know at least one person (quite possibly themselves) who has had some kind of brush with emigration.[*] It seems that everyone is 'at it'!

---

[*] With the possible exception of really old people – although my 95-year-old grandma knows 'a nice girl from the village who moved to Russia'!

When I started researching this book, I came across a UK survey[2] which had some pretty surprising stats. Instead of focusing on the number of people who *had* emigrated, it was more concerned with those who were *thinking* of emigrating and it appears there are quite a few of you. In fact a whopping 33 per cent of British females said that they would actually 'consider emigrating'. That represents one third of the female population! In other words, if you are reading this book while travelling to work, observe your fellow female commuters and understand that one in three of them is only pretending to read that crumpled copy of *The Daily Mail*, while secretly daydreaming about clearing off to another country.

And you, so it seems, are one of them!

According to the number crunchers, three per cent of the world's population (that's around 200 million people in layman's terms) are living somewhere other than their home country.[3] And as for the Brits, it's been estimated that there are around 5.5 million of us living abroad on a long-term basis.[4] In 2009, movement began to slow, but even with the global financial climate being as chilly as it is, people are still looking for 'something more' – a brighter life, a better life...and maybe one that's a three-minute walk to the beach.

And you thought you were the only one who felt like escaping! Didn't we all?

But why are so many of us on the move these days? Why are Sensible Girls emigrating elegantly (or at least thinking about it)? Abandoning family and friends, jobs and homes and moving abroad? In fact, why did you start reading this book in the first place, flicking through its pages wondering whether it might be the key to helping you overcome your reservations about leaving the country? Why indeed?

If you haven't already noticed, I'm afraid there is going to be a fair amount of audience participation while reading this book, so let's move on to the next exercise.

Please read through the following statements and tick any that apply to you.

• I am thinking about emigrating.	✔
• I would like to improve my lifestyle, which has become a bit rubbish.‡	
• I would like to spend as much time with my partner as I do with the passengers I stand next to on the bus/tube/train twice a day.	
• I would like to have a partner.	
• I would like to have the time and energy to cook an evening meal from scratch, without purchasing a single pre-prepared, pre-cooked, pre-packed item from Marks & Spencer.	
• On seeing the sun, I would like to remain rational and calm, rather than dashing out and burning myself to a crisp for fear of never feeling its warmth on my white flesh again.	

---

‡ Feel free to substitute the word 'rubbish' with: irritating, boring, dull, cold, stressful, miserable, unfulfilling, uneventful, depressing, annoying, and so forth.

• I would like to find a parking space.	
• I would like to be able to afford a modest house, in a decent area that has a bigger floor plan than the office lavatory.	
• I would like to get more for my money.	
• I would like to enjoy life on a day-to-day basis, rather than living from one holiday to the next.	
• I would like my thighs to shrink.	
• I would like a 'great job' rather than a 'fabulous career' and feel that 'office ambition' is an overrated sport.	
• I would like it to stop raining.	
• I would like to get enthusiastic about something OTHER than purchasing a new pair of shoes.	
• I would like to start a new life, experience new things, have a loving relationship, babies, a veggie patch, a furry pet that doesn't smell...	

OK, so you get the point. You've probably ticked quite a few of the statements, which is no surprise as emigration surveys posing the question 'why do you want to emigrate?' list the following reasons (in no particular order).

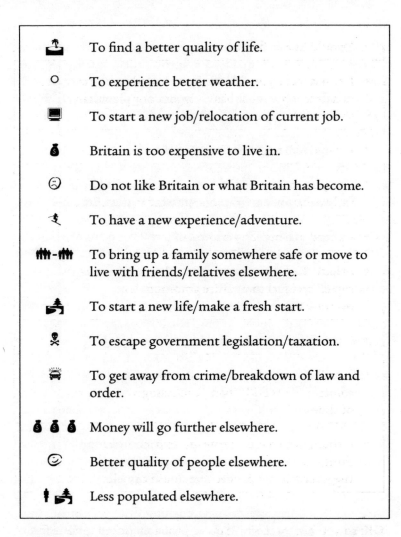

To find a better quality of life.

To experience better weather.

To start a new job/relocation of current job.

Britain is too expensive to live in.

Do not like Britain or what Britain has become.

To have a new experience/adventure.

To bring up a family somewhere safe or move to live with friends/relatives elsewhere.

To start a new life/make a fresh start.

To escape government legislation/taxation.

To get away from crime/breakdown of law and order.

Money will go further elsewhere.

Better quality of people elsewhere.

Less populated elsewhere.

'Emigration used to be mainly [a way] for people to earn more money,' say Sabina Eijkman and Nynke Bruinsma, co-founders of a company called The Expat Coaches,[6] who coach people through the various stages of emigration. 'Nowadays we [find] people are moving abroad to improve their quality of life. Stressful, demanding jobs, lack of time, social pressure to succeed, multicultural society issues, political aspects, changing environment, the weather...are all now reasons to consider emigration.'

Generally speaking, Brits moving abroad do so for the 'pull' factors rather than the 'push' ones. In other words, contrary to popular belief, not everyone lists 'The UK is rubbish' as their primary reason for emigrating. Although most Sensible Girls would be the first to admit they have a few 'issues' with Blighty (the crappy weather, rising crime and a recession...to name but a few), they still focus on the positive potential of what their new country has to offer (e.g. warmer climate, better lifestyles) rather than blindly running away from the negatives.

So we've established that you need a few changes in your life, but does that really mean upping sticks, packing your bags and leaving this green and pleasant land? I mean, *emigrating*...isn't that a bit drastic? Couldn't you just go for a spray-on tan and have a quick flick through the job section of the *Evening Standard* instead?

Admittedly, when life changes are afoot, not everyone moves overseas. Some people simply move to bigger houses in the countryside – which, according to TV relocation programmes, has a wealth of rundown barns in desperate need of a makeover – and commute. Some people give up on city life altogether and open B&Bs by the sea and slave over a full English fry-up each morning. But many of us are branching out ever further and fleeing the UK altogether. What was once a monumental decision has been downsized to something that (given the right planning) we can realistically try out and see how we get on.

Judging by all the relocation programmes that have sprung up on the telly over the last few years, there appears to be a rumbling in the suburbs, an overall feeling of discontent that is brewing in urban England. Mark Chapman, series producer of various Tiger Aspect relocation shows such as *A Place In...*(Spain, France, Slovakia, etc.)[7] explains:

'I think undoubtedly [that] shows like *A Place in the Sun* make it look fun to buy and move abroad. The general sense is that you can get something far more idyllic or grand for your money, and still have change to enjoy yourself. But I think there is also something fundamentally intriguing to people about starting a new life somewhere else.

'The general feeling in the UK is that it's an incredibly expensive place to live, and becoming more and more restrictive and controlled. I think people feel they are freer when abroad, perhaps because they don't quite understand the culture, and are therefore able to live a kind of holiday existence.'

We need to make some changes. The endless trips to Topshop to find that perfect Chloé rip-off, the girlie chats over a bottle of wine and the string of holidays to try to keep that year-round tan, while still being fabulous are not enough to satisfy a Sensible Girl who wants to broaden her horizons. We love our lives and we're quite happy with *who* we are, but some of us feel that it is time to start digging ourselves out of any comfortable (or uncomfortable) ruts before it's too late.

Priorities are shifting. Renting on Portobello Road used to be a wonderful idea; now it's just noisy and claustrophobic, not to mention the fact that you resent paying a small fortune for the privilege of living in a carpeted pigeon hole.

No space,

no time,

no change,

no fresh air.

We all work so hard that when we have a nanosecond of time off, we party, shop, exercise and drink wine (not necessarily in that order) even harder to make ourselves feel better about the huge effort we are putting into our lives. The merry-go-round speeds up at an alarming rate and before you know it you're clinging on too tight to jump off.

So how do you pluck up the courage to let go and actually jump? After all, it's all very well *wanting* to emigrate, but as you are now acutely aware, the gap between 'wanting to' and actually 'doing it' is rather large. Counselling psychologist Lisa Palmer[8] explains:

'Deciding whether to emigrate or not can be stressful. This is because human beings need security and yet they also crave autonomy and exploration. This "contradiction of needs" means that we perform a type of mental balancing act throughout the course of our lives. So when the idea of emigration comes along, we are forced to make a decision that requires us to leave everything that supports that security behind, throwing our balance off kilter, and this is intrinsically stressful.'

So if deciding to emigrate is so tricky, how do we overcome these mental barriers that hold us back?

'Give yourself plenty of time,' is Lisa's first piece of advice. 'Allow yourself the opportunity to grieve for what you are going to miss and leave behind. But balance this with your desire to explore what new frontiers and opportunities await you overseas. Emigrating is a complex human adjustment process that you just need to come to terms with before going ahead and actually doing it.'

The word 'emigrate' sounds like it belongs in a dusty old school book. Taken (as you'd guess) from the verb to migrate, it conjures up images of flocks of big honking geese flying from one country to the next, or sepia images of stern-faced families boarding ships at Southampton docks, carrying their worldly belongings in trunks, never to return. It makes you feel like you might be getting a headache just thinking about it, but that could just be because it's next to 'migraine' in the dictionary. Anyway, whatever the word 'emigrate' means to you, the phrase 'living abroad for a while' certainly doesn't feel quite as scary. And that's the point; it shouldn't.

It's not that long ago since families and convicts alike were being shipped off to distant lands. Our grandparents might remember the 'Ten Pound Poms'; Brits who were actually paid to go and live in Australia (oh, the irony!). When someone emigrated back then, there was rarely anything temporary about it. Changing one's mind back then and deciding to return home (otherwise known as 'ping pomming') was a lot more tricky than it is now.

Us girls are more transient, affluent and independent than our great-grandmothers were. Which means we can do more of 'what we want', 'when we want', 'WHERE we want'! A recent survey[9] estimates that roughly seven million British nationals are pootling around outside the UK's borders at any one time and in 2007 we made over 69.5 million trips overseas[10] (which works out at more than one per person). In amongst these Brits abroad is a special breed of traveller. A breed that, over the past few decades, has partied like it's 1999 on remote tropical islands, and drunk and 'slept' its way across entire continents. I am, of course, talking about the ubiquitous backpacker.

Back in the olden days, our parents' generation considered backpacking a novelty, whereas now, even with the credit crunch snapping at our heels, a gap year is positively encouraged. In 2005, just over 31,000 British students deferred their entries to university[11] – no prizes for guessing what the vast majority of them would be getting up to during their year off! In 2009, finding the finances to fund a foreign sojourn might be a bit more challenging, but that doesn't seem to have quelled Sensible Girls' wanderlust.

Data shows[12] that this free-minded mentality will only get stronger as each generation that was 'born to backpack', grows towards middle age. Britons aged between 18 and 24 are twice as likely to want to emigrate in the near future, than those of middle age. Which means that, at some point in their lives, Sensible Girls of the future will be far more likely to have a crack at living somewhere other than the UK.

In simple terms, the evolution of emigrating for the Sensible 'Gal on the go' looks something like this:

Step One – Holidaying with Mum and Dad somewhere sunny on the Med.

↓

Step Two – Backpacking with best mate as far away as possible from home.

↓

Step Three – Emigrating with 'Lord only knows who' to 'Lord only knows where'.

These broadening horizons are affecting our current attitudes towards working and living abroad. More people are trying it and, as we now know, even more people are *thinking* about trying it

After all, the *Oxford English Dictionary*'s definition of 'emigrate' does not say 'to leave a country to go and settle in another for at least ten years even if you don't like it and you miss your mum'. No, you can stay for as long as you want. Follow a few sensible rules (which we will go into shortly) and you can pretty much please yourself, but you're not going to get there without putting in a bit of effort.

As with everything in life, it's a case of mind over matter. You just need to dig out a little bit of self-belief. It's all about taking that first step and going for it, and let's face it, you've done that already by choosing to read this book. After all, you could be reading *Bricklaying for Idiots* or *Shout Your Way into Public Speaking* – but you're not. So, however you look at it, that first step is long gone and we're currently focusing on step number two: being proactive.

Now if you've been daydreaming about living abroad for some time, I would like to be very clear about what 'being proactive' means. Watching relocation programmes on TV and moaning that 'they're just *so* lucky' is not actually being proactive. Neither is attending a travel fair or emigration forum, getting lots of useful information and then shoving it, unread, in a pile at the back of your wardrobe. What you're actually doing there is SOD ALL. You're just making token gestures towards your cause. Either that or you're waiting for someone to come along and do it all for you!

And I hate to disappoint you, but they won't. It's all up to you, I'm afraid. When it comes to successfully negotiating your emigration, you can't be half-hearted about anything – you've got to grab the 'emigrating horns' firmly in both hands, take a deep breath and hang on for dear life.

Lesley Sumner,[13] who is used to coaxing the answers out of confused souls and guiding them gently towards their goals, in her former career as a life coach, strongly believes that the first step can often be the hardest:

'Clients will often approach me with an overall feeling of dissatisfaction...but they're not quite sure why or what to do about it. They've reached a point in their life when the burning questions is: "Is this *it* for the rest of my life?"'

'The best trick I would suggest when trying to decide whether you wish to emigrate or not is to use a visualisation technique often employed by life coaches. Picture yourself living abroad in five years' time...and then picture yourself staying in the UK in five years' time. What does each picture look like? How does it feel? Are you happy? Do you have any regrets? Then do the same for 10 years. This usually helps to clarify the dilemma.'

Meanwhile Paul Beasley, editor of *Emigrate ↗ Magazine*,[14] also says that you should be asking yourself some tough questions:

'Emigration is challenging, heart-rending, bold, adventurous, frightening, risky and life-changing[...]. Clearly, there's nothing wrong with being perfectly positive about the plus points of emigrating, but you should ensure that a real decision-making process takes place.'

So it's time to have a little tête-à-tête with yourself and answer a few tough questions:

?

Are you super-sure that you will be able to cope with emigrating?

Would a 'Life Tweak', (such as moving house, changing jobs) be a better solution, rather than full blown Emigration?

Do you make friends easily?

How have you coped with starting a new job or moving house in the past?

Are you a creature of habit, settled into a cosy routine... and if so, how will you cope if that is taken away from you?

How will you manage without the immediate support of family and friends?

If you have a partner, is he or she ready to make a big move too?

And the biggest question of all

...how do you cope with change?

Try not to get too upset if these kind of questions freak you out. 'Should you be having doubts, this doesn't mean you must abandon your dreams right here and now,' says Paul. 'Rather, it's better to have doubts now and overcome them sensibly than to rush into thoughtless emigration only to have doubts several thousand miles – and several thousand pounds – down the line.[15]'

It's only natural to have doubts buzzing around your head when it comes to deciding whether to emigrate or not. So long as you think things through properly, you will come up with the right answer. And when you do – once you're comfortable with your decision, once you've accepted that you are going to emigrate – everything *will* start falling into place.

That's not to say that things are going to be easy, because they won't be, but if you tackle one obstacle at a time you'll find yourself waving goodbye in the departure lounge before you know it! All you need is a bit of confidence and an Escape Plan. So, stop wondering, worrying or whingeing and start working out what it is that you're really looking for.

OK, it's all about visualisation. Look at the following pictures and select the one that most closely represents your desired future.

A)

B)

C)

A) Boo! Step away from the book and get back to the office. You're not going anywhere just yet.

B) Yay! Continue to the next chapter and begin your escape.

C) Right-oh – you weren't really paying attention there were you? Re-read Chapter 1 and try again!

CHAPTER 2
WHAT'S YOUR 'SENSIBLE STATUS'?

Seize the moment.
Remember all those women on the 'Titanic' who waved off the dessert cart.
ERMA BOMBECK[1]

Before we go any further with your emigration planning, you need to take a close look at yourself and establish exactly *who* you are.

Don't worry, we're not talking in-depth psychoanalysis – just the basics will do. You see, before we can proceed, we need to be very clear about your Sensible circumstances as they will affect exactly how you manage your emigration.

For example:

* Are you in a meaningful relationship – or indeed in an unmeaningful one?
* Are you an independent career chick or a team-playing office worker?
* Are you a twenty-something housewife who likes to play it safe or a sixty-something grandmother who's a bit of a thrill-seeker?
* Do you plan to undertake this alone or with a boyfriend, girlfriend, husband, ex, child, brood or pet canary?
* Are you moving away from your family and friends or into their welcoming bosom?
* Are you a spring chicken starting a new life or a mature bird finishing off an old one?

'Moving abroad is a big challenge,' agree Sabina Eijkman and Nynke Bruinsma, co-founders of The Expat Coaches.[2] 'Making the most of it is absolutely based on knowing *who* you are, what you want and focusing on getting there. To make a success of emigration, women have to know themselves. If a woman knows what makes her 'tick' (being a mum, being a housewife, working part-time or full-time, volunteering, retiring, being a globetrotter, etc.) she can create her new life abroad.'

While it's a given that each person's experience of moving abroad will be very different, it can't be denied that ultimately we're all a big bunch of clichés – so the chances are that you will fall into one (or more) of the following categories.

♀ × ? = 🌐

1. SENSIBLE AND SINGLE

Nice and simple, just how we like it.

If you are Sensible and Single, you will be an independent, free-thinking young lady who has the innate sense that there is more to life that what you are currently experiencing. And for this reason alone, you have every intention of getting out there and finding it.

Without wishing to state the obvious, you only have yourself to deal with here. There is no one else for you to worry about, no one to try to persuade and no one to feel responsible for. You might not always appreciate the autonomous approach, but speak to anyone trying to win over a Reluctant Partner* and you will see the complicated path they tread when trying to reach their dream destination.

Partners can throw up all kinds of emotional baggage; they could secretly be loathing the idea of emigration, but are going ahead with it to keep the peace. They could be planning on

---

* Read on...you'll meet him a bit later.

dumping their significant other once they're settled in Their New Country. The possibilities are endless – and quite frankly, not your concern, which is why it is great to be planning your single-handed escape.

You begin to realise how much pressure has been avoided by being single. You can please yourself, pick where you want to live, go when you want to go and, of course, change your mind a hundred times if you want to. It can actually be a very liberating experience.

That said, you still might wish you had a big strapping bloke to hold your hand during this rather intimidating journey, but you really don't need one. Instead, consider the option of getting yourself a nice 'new one' once you get there. For the key thing that will really make you fall in love with YNC is falling in love. Believe me, it's the perfect way to settle in and feel at home. Plus a new partner will open a myriad of social and practical doors.

If you've got bored of waiting for Mr Right to sweep you off your feet in the UK, maybe it is time to carbonate your life and shake things up a bit. After all, he doesn't appear to be on your bus or tube in the morning, or in your local pub, or pushing his squeaky trolley around Waitrose...so why hang around? Just get out your map and start looking a bit further afield!

Being Sensible and Single doesn't necessarily mean to say you will be emigrating on your own – just without a partner tagging along. Going 'back to your roots' is a common relocation reason for Sensible Girls, many of whom want to move into the loving bosom of their 'foreign family'. Maybe your mum has moved back to Jamaica and you want to join her, or your auntie lives in Portugal and you've always quite fancied living there. Globalisation has led to families becoming more dispersed around the world, and it is becoming increasingly easy to visit them, stay with them or indeed *live* with them. So if you're lucky enough to be moving in with loved ones, enjoy (and read further benefits which can apply to you in 'Going Out with Johnny Foreigner').

A well-trodden route for Sensible Singles is along the career path. Statistics show[3] that the majority of Brits who leave the UK do so to seek employment abroad, making it a key factor of emigration. Being single allows you to selfishly devote your entire being to succeeding in such a move. You can throw yourself in head first and accept every social invitation without giving a second thought to anyone else. And with such drive and focus you should find yourself moving up that work ladder (as well as the social one) as quickly and fabulously as possible.

Another benefit of being single that Sensible Girls experience when moving abroad is that they often make friends a lot more quickly than Sensible Couples. I know you probably expect the opposite to happen and fear that you will soon become known as the Sad Little British Girl or Billy No-Mates, but think again. As any backpacker will remind you, it can be far easier to make friends if you are on your own as you are forced into being pro-active about the whole socialising scene and give off a more open, friendly kind of vibe.

While it is understandable to feel apprehensive about going it alone, try to concentrate on the positive rather than the negative points of being a single gal. Imagine the sense of achievement you will experience. In a few months' time, you will move to a new country, make a whole bunch of new friends, meet prospective new boyfriends and have a lot of fun in the process.

So next time you're stuck in that 8.30am traffic jam, ask yourself what's so bad about that?

2. GOING OUT WITH A SENSIBLE CHAP†

Lucky you, this is also a great position to be in if you are planning to move abroad. You are about to experience something wonderful and exciting with the person you love. And, on a more practical note, living costs are instantly halved and you get someone to carry your luggage – hurrah!

You are fortunate enough to have someone who will look after you (and vice-versa) through this life-changing experience and this is a huge confidence-builder in itself. Just be prepared for a few tough patches along the way. You not only need to be committed to your cause, but also to each other. Your relationship has to be strong, or you may not survive the plethora of experiences and emotions you are about to go through. But the trade-off is that once you start working through emigration's challenges, your relationship should strengthen and grow.

And, speaking of commitment, are you and your Sensible Chap married? If not, would you like to be? It's probably not a question you fancy answering at this precise moment in time, as

---

† Or 'Chapess'. Obviously Sensible Gay Girls are included in the mix, but it was just a lot easier to refer to all partners as being male rather than sounding overly PC and running through all the options each time.

you've got enough to be thinking about. But if wedding bells *are* on the cards, you should sit down and have a quick chat about where and when you would like to tie the knot, as emigrating has an annoying habit of complicating things.

If you were thinking of getting hitched in YNC, you could, for example, face the prospect of having a somewhat depleted guest list because of distance, cost, elderly relatives having problems with flying, etc. On the other hand, YNC could be paradise and turn your dreams of a fabulous beach wedding into reality!

Likewise, if you were thinking of organising your wedding from YNC so that you can return to the UK for your big day, another set of challenges arises, such as viewing venues, choosing outfits (without your mum and best mate to help) and, if you were thinking of a church wedding, living in the parish for the required amount of time before you can legally tie the knot. All food for thought. There is always the option of doing the deed before you leave, which would get the aforementioned complications out of the way. But this is only an option if you allow enough time to fit everything in *comfortably*, without completely losing the plot.

Anyway, rather than get too bogged down in the minutiae of your wedding plans, just make sure you consider your options. In the meantime, if he's 'your man' and you love him, it doesn't matter if your drunken conversations about moving to New Zealand were...well, drunken conversations. If you're both really serious about escaping, it's time to get moving!

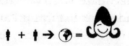

3. GOING OUT WITH A RELUCTANT PARTNER

Oh dear. This can be tough and is one of the most common reasons why some Sensible Girls do *not* emigrate. If you are sensing that your other half is not as enthusiastic about emigrating as you are, sadly you may be the unsuspecting owner of a Reluctant Partner.

Reluctant Partners can be split into two groups. The ones that will eventually (after a moderate amount of nonsense) succumb to the lure of foreign shores and emigrate with you. And the ones that (after a moderate amount of nonsense) will succumb to the lure of their local pub and not budge an inch. The trick is identifying which type of partner you own, and it is better to do this sooner rather than later.

When trying to negotiate your way through this potential minefield and persuade your Reluctant Partner that any shot at future happiness lies in another country, feel free to use some of the following tried and trusted techniques.

Helpful hints for dealing with a Reluctant Partner

Stick to your guns
VERY IMPORTANT if you are to succeed.

Surreptitious observation
As we've already established, you could be the owner of a
Reluctant Partner who will (in time) change his mind
and move abroad with you. So you will need to monitor
his behaviour and give him a time limit to comply. It is
important that you do not *tell* him this time limit‡ as it
might affect his willingness to 'play nicely'.

Show him the money
A large number of Reluctant Partners experience a change
of mind, not because of a sudden urge to live abroad but
because of MONEY! A well-paid relocation package can be
a huge incentive to anyone's career. Add to that a contract
with an end date (thus enabling the co-operating couple
the prospect of returning to the Motherland) and you've
got yourself an escape plan. Some move abroad for the love
of a foreign land; others for a large wad of cash. Whatever
the reason, if it gets you from A to B – don't knock it!

Don't mistake the definition of compromise
There is the obvious option of compromise. But make
no mistake, this does not mean staying put and seeing if
your wanderlust passes ('she'll get over it'). That's just
you compromising yourself. 'Try living abroad for a year
and if it doesn't work, we can move back' could be

---

‡   More than a week, less than six months.

considered a compromise; it just depends on how you look at things. The two of you need to make equal sacrifices and be open to each other's ambitions for the future.

Show him that you respect his reasons for not wanting to go
If he feels invalidated and misunderstood, he's not going to budge. But if you take the time to hear his reasoning, maybe he will listen to yours and then you can have a nice adult conversation and talk things through together.

Show him that you are serious
Keep on moving with your own plans. Don't just wait for him to change his mind. If he sees any hesitation in your emigrating ambitions – he'll realise that he stands a chance of staying put and will make no effort whatsoever.

Get him interested...it's not just all about you!
As you are beginning to learn, you can push and shove all you like, but in order to get this boy moving he needs to *want* to go. While you are steadfast in your mission to move abroad, empathise with his decision-making process too. Margaret Malewski, author of *GenXpat: The Young Professional's Guide to Making a Successful Life Abroad*,[4] believes that relocation can cause an enormous amount of stress to a partner who is not the instigator of the move. And the only way to encourage him to budge is to make sure he has a 'strong personal interest in the relocation' as well as a belief that 'he can achieve his objectives as well as yours'.

If he has not budged an inch within your said time limit – is it time to kiss him goodbye?§

Ouch! Well, is it? If you are reading this with a wobbly lip and feel totally distraught at the prospect of leaving your beloved in order to jump ship and start anew, perhaps you need to reconsider things. Maybe the compromise could lie in a different part of this country to begin with or even a different part of town? Changes need to be made and you must try to stay true to your dreams during this rather messy process.

The longer you leave it, the harder the decision will be

If you are really serious about escaping, you need to strike while the iron's hot! As my fairy tale has already illustrated, the end result is usually inevitable and if you're brutally honest you know deep down whether he's a 'goer' or a 'stayer', but it's how quickly you reach this conclusion that's important.

DO NOT become a 'What If' Girl

On the whole, we only regret the things in life we don't do – ask any Sensible Grandma. There are couples out there who consist of one silent partner who still secretly dreams of the opportunity that passed him or her by, the chance of finding Their New Country to having a go at 'living the dream'.

So, all I'm asking is that you take your dreams seriously and don't just shove them to the back of your mind and try to forget about them.

---

§ If you are already married to this person, feel free to substitute the words 'kiss him goodbye' with 'grind him down'. Sorry, boys!

Some may find this rather extreme, but another way of describing the predicament you're in is to liken it to a couple who have opposing views about wanting children. If you want babies, but your partner doesn't, sooner or later this issue will have to be addressed. You might love one another deeply, but if neither of you can budge on the topic, you may feel the need to move on and find someone who does want kids...or in your case someone who wants to emigrate.

Reluctant Partners are to Sensible Emigrating Girls what icebergs were to the *Titanic*, so be watchful and try to avoid ever bumping into one if you can possibly help it.

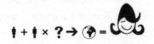

4. THE RELUCTANT GIRL

Sometimes it can be the boys who are up for it rather than the girls. For example, at any one time there can be around 35,000 members of the UK forces stationed abroad,[5] which means there are a lot of Sensible Wives and Girlfriends out there[¶] who are trying to get their heads round moving to foreign postings.

¶ Or of course Sensible Boyfriends and Husbands.

Likewise, your partner might be offered a business opportunity overseas that he just can't turn down. Becoming a 'tailing spouse' (a term used amongst expats – which sounds rather like an unusual breed of rodent!) can be tough.

'In the case of women following their husbands abroad, they sometimes give up their own career in their home country,' say Sabina and Nynke from The Expat Coaches.[6] 'When women follow their husbands, they feel like they have to leave everything behind. They don't know IF and HOW they can have a career abroad and in the case of expat families, there are also children involved [see The Sensible Mummy, page 33] which means the mother has to deal with the family issues as well.'

With so much to think about, you need to clear your head and work out what YOU are looking for.

Just like the boys, you can either be a Negative Nancy and block out all attempts at discussing emigration, or you can at least consider it as a viable option. Some Sensible Young Ladies can sway from one viewpoint to the other. And some can perform amazing trapeze acts where they swing back and forth[**] while having a mild nervous breakdown. The key is to keep communication open with your loved one and talk things through.

Helpful hints if YOU are the Reluctant Partner

Don't panic
Yes, it's scary, but try to stay calm and discuss things

[**] They want to go...they don't want to go...they want to go...they don't want to go.

openly and sensibly with your partner. You do not want to develop Bunny-In-Headlights Syndrome.

Take the second step
Well, you're reading this book so there must be a small part of you that is interested in emigrating. Nurture this little seed as it may grow to be something very exciting.

Appreciate that we're not all on the same page at the same time
Some people are quicker readers than others, so if it takes you a little while to reach the bit that says 'yep – I want to emigrate' or 'nope – I don't', that's fine. Be patient with yourself; just keep on reading.

Start writing lists
While your partner is busy writing wish lists, researching your potential new country and generally behaving like an overexcited Labrador, you need to start quietly writing your own lists:

- why you **want** to stay in the UK;
- why you **don't want** to live in Proposed New Country;
- why you **might like** to leave the UK;
- why you **might like** to live in Proposed New Country.

The key is to write positive things down under each heading, rather than sticking your bottom lip out and penning a thesis entitled: 'Humpf! I don't want to go because...'

Factor an escape plan within your Escape Plan
Yes, it's a bit confusing. But this will act like a security
blanket if you're on the verge of deciding to give it a go
but need an extra bit of persuasion. Knowing that, if all
else fails you can get back to Blighty and return to your
old life, might just give you the strength to move away
from it in the first place.

You don't have to go if you don't want to
If you decide that you definitely, categorically,
unquestionably do NOT want to go...DON'T. Starting a
new life in a new country is hard enough, especially if
you don't actually want to be there.

Depending on where you are in your relationship, be
prepared to accept the consequences that your decision
brings. It's a bit scary but you must be true to yourself
and so does your partner.

...but if you do want to go!
If there is still a small part of you that is interested in
emigrating, even if it is so miniscule it can't be detected
by the human eye...GO FOR IT. You don't know if you
don't try.††

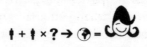

---

†† All accusations of bias are fully acknowledged.

5. GOING OUT WITH JOHNNY FOREIGNER

Easy peasy lemon squeezy!

One of *the* key elements of a successful emigration is integrating into YNC and statistics prove that this is most likely to be achieved when a Sensible Girl emigrates with a partner who is a national of the host country. So dating Johnny can give you a ginormous head start when it comes to the practicalities of emigrating.

Whether you are already living in his country or in the throes of a long-distance relationship (LDR), your dual-nationality-date could make your emigration experience much easier: visas and other paperwork may be more easily obtainable if you are in a de-facto relationship (see Chapter 6), finding your way around once you're there won't be a problem, you will probably have his friends and family for support, you'll get free language tuition if necessary, a place to stay when you arrive, he can help you deal with inevitable culture shock...the list goes on.

Be prepared to be a little overwhelmed when you first arrive in YNC. The experience of falling into a new life with an all-singing, all-dancing, brand new foreign family can take some getting used to (complete with nagging mother-in-law, creepy uncle and squawking nieces). This can make you feel a little torn, as you want to be the perfect new arrival into the foreign fold, but don't want to lose your sanity trying to ingratiate yourself to your new hosts. If you keep in mind that this arrangement is temporary and make sure that your partner is sensitive to the situation, you'll get through it.

Being a Sensible Girl yourself, I am of course working on the assumption that you have already met your Johnny Foreigner lover and are not about to uproot your life in the UK after a three-week Internet romance with a Prince Charming who turns out to be a pre-pubescent computer nerd from Woop Woop.

And, speaking of relationships coming to an end, I feel we should touch briefly on what you would do if (heaven forbid) you and your partner split up once you live in YNC. It may be a horrid thought, but it is also one of the main reasons for people having to move back to the UK. Now I'm not suggesting you buy a spare beach house or start opening secret Swiss bank accounts, but be sensible and try to reduce the danger of you having to leave the country if things go wrong between you.

6. THE SENSIBLE MUMMY

Whether you are single, de facto or married to Mr Wonderful, there is another little issue that might affect your willingness to throw everything in a bag and move to the Tropics – kids!

Finding somewhere fabulous to bring up a family is a *big* reason why Brits move abroad. And there is no reason why children can't benefit hugely from the experiences of living in another country, so long as their parents are sensitive to their needs and take their child's feelings and futures into consideration as much as their own.

As this book focuses on persuading the 'big kids' to emigrate, it would be very wise to arm yourself with some more detailed literature on the joys of emigrating with the little ones, but keep a few of the following things in mind when getting things started.

Your main concern will be your child's health and schooling and, as a general rule, the younger your child is, the easier they will adjust to going to school in a new country. The closer to puberty, the harder it becomes (although as always with kids, there are exceptions to the rule). Where possible, try to contact the education authority or schools information service in YNC through government websites as soon as possible so you have plenty of time to get your head round foreign application processes. Be aware that not all countries have free state-funded education. Find out what your child will be entitled to and work out whether you need to focus on state or private schooling and if an English-speaking international school is a viable option.

Never underestimate the effect that emigration has on a child (that's not to say it's negative). Helping your kids (whatever age group) acclimatise into YNC means giving them some kind of closure when leaving the UK and at the same time keeping some form of their UK routine alive while living abroad. You're trying to make the transition from one country to the next both exciting and seamless – all at the same time! Even if you're not sure what's going to happen in YNC, give them some kind of direction when planning your foreign future as they need security. And don't forget that, for a five year old, 12 months seems a lot longer than it does to an adult, so you will need to deal with their settling-in process differently from your own.

The best thing you can do at this stage is to really try to get your kids involved in the whole emigration process so that if you do decide to take the leap of faith and live overseas, you will feel confident that you're doing what's best for *everyone* in the family.[††]

♀ + ⛹ → 🌍 = 😊

[††] And give the grandparents a bit of thought too, as the effects of taking their little bundles of joy to another country can be upsetting for them (and tricky for you if they offered a champion babysitting service).

7. THE SENSIBLE SENIOR

Even though this book is primarily aimed at younger Sensible Girls, there may be the odd Sensible Senior flicking through these pages and seeing what this emigrating malarkey is all about.

Well, you are in good company, as the population of Grey Nomads roaming this planet is on the rise.

The UK Government dishes out a huge amount of its pension payments overseas (last count – to an estimated one million pensioners living abroad). Sensible Seniors retiring to the Costa Del-What-Not and beyond have been heading out there in their droves, with one set of projections totalling more than 1.8 million oldies (that's 13.2 per cent of the UK's retired population) moving overseas by 2025...increasing to a whopping 3.3 million by 2050.[7] Now whether these OAP predictions come into fruition or not, the point is that going for a wander around the world and getting a bit of sun on your bones is no longer reserved for the under-25s.

Maybe you want to emigrate permanently, or simply pop over to sunny Spain and take refuge from those perishing British winters for a few months each year. Maybe children or grandchildren are the prime reason for your newly discovered wanderlust. Or you simply want a bit of adventure now that you've finally hit retirement. No matter what the reason, the process can seem like an uphill struggle and one that you're not sure whether you've got the energy to embark on.

Stick with it and remind yourself of all those rather lovely hidden extras. Depending on where you're aiming for, you can often expect lower living costs and better living environments (which put you in very good stead for a healthy and wealthy retirement).

However, as with all Sensible Emigrating Girls, there will be paperwork to fill in. It is imperative that you research what benefits and entitlements you can expect to receive from YNC and more importantly what welfare rights and pension access you have from the UK once abroad.

Find out about healthcare costs in YNC and look into health insurance to cover private medical and dental treatment as well as medical repatriation to the UK. Do this *before* you emigrate, rather than once you get there as foreign bureaucracy can be a slippery fish to get a hold of and sadly there are an increasing number of casualties who find themselves in a financial no man's land unable to claim certain benefits from either country once they have moved.

Horror stories aside, Grey Nomads lead the way in emigrating to such places as Southern Europe, so why not follow in their footsteps? Who cares if you have four grandchildren, two cats and a bionic hip? That doesn't mean to say that you can't go and play in the foreign sunshine with everyone else!

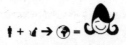

OK, no doubt there will be the odd Sensible Girl reading this who doesn't quite fall neatly into any particular category – but you get the gist.

You see, the reason I want to establish what kind of a girl you are and what commitments you have is so that I can best communicate the following important fact:

**ALL SENSIBLE GIRLS CAN EMIGRATE
IF THEY REALLY WANT TO.**

Likewise, anyone can come up with a list of reasons why they *can't* emigrate.§§ People often hide behind excuses because they're scared: 'Oh I'd love to move to the States, but my boyfriend doesn't want to' or 'I'd jump at the chance to live in Spain, but we've got the baby now', when what they really mean is: 'I'm sure we'd be fine taking the baby, but I'm a bit nervous', or 'I could probably persuade my boyfriend to move abroad, but I'm not sure I dare go myself!'.

The path to living in a new country is tricky and, yes, it's strewn with obstacles and problems, but isn't that the case with anything in life – moving house, starting a new job, organising a spectacular dinner party? Don't underestimate yourself and think that the whole thing is out of your reach, because it really isn't. Family, partners, kids, friends, pets...you can hide behind these loved ones and let them prevent you from having a go, or you can enlist their help and advice and get on with it. You just need to have a plan, be disciplined and work confidently towards your goal.

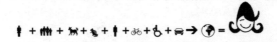

OK, less of the heavy stuff, let's get started.

---

§§ Thus making them not sensible.

CHAPTER 3

GETTING STARTED

So you've FINALLY decided to give it a go.

You're going to emigrate. That's fantastic! How do you feel? I remember experiencing a multitude of emotions once my partner and I finally, after months of deliberation, decided to go for it. They ranged from happiness, excitement, anticipation and relief to total panic. I experienced a similar set of emotions many years earlier, when schoolfriends persuaded me to get on an extremely large rollercoaster I had been eyeing up all day. I jumped on while making comments like 'Oh my God, what am I doing?', had a grin the size of a stoned Cheshire cat's and, amidst the hilarity and excitement, was absolutely petrified.

But, after one vertical drop, two loop-the-loops and me laughing so much I nearly peed my pants, the ride was over – and I was ecstatic! Primarily because I was alive (and my pants were dry!), but also because I had actually DONE IT. I had felt the fear and done it anyway (to flog a well-worn self-help phrase) and that is exactly what you are about to do.

'Emigration is a big thing,' say Sabina and Nynke, our Expat Coaches.[1] 'It is a continuous battle between what it is you're leaving behind and what it is that you think you're going to get so, needless to say, preparation is important.'

In the last chapter, we established WHO you are, but before working out WHERE you plan to emigrate, we need to determine exactly WHAT it is that you are looking for – and in order to do that, you need to prepare your Wish List.

This is a very important list, so you must write it in a suitable environment conducive to positive thinking. You will require the following:

- **one quiet table** in local drinking establishment (no restaurants as food will prove distracting);
- **one notepad/piece of paper** (no empty ciggy packs, drinking mats etc. – too limiting, think big!);
- **one pencil** (with a rubber on the end – for changing one's mind);
- **a substantial quantity of alcohol**. More than a glass, less than a litre (remember that you need to be lucid, not trolleyed);
- **one free evening** (with partner – if you own one and they are coming with you).

Sensible Single Girls can substitute a local drinking establishment for the sofa (if they prefer not to drink alone): just make sure the TV is turned off. Sensible Mums just need to find some elusive quiet time wherever and whenever they can grab it.

When writing your Wish List, it is tempting to involve 'the girls' at this stage, but it is really important to exclude friends for the moment. While they are obviously all lovely and kind, they have their own agendas and may influence yours unintentionally. E.g. 'Oooh, wouldn't it be great if we *both* went to Costa Rica and lived in the Spider Monkey rescue centre together' or 'Oh, but I wanted you to be my bridesmaid this summer. Can't you go next year?'.

By all means get your friends on board once you have decided what it is you're aiming for (who knows, someone might want to come with you), but first get your uncontaminated, uninfluenced Wish List in writing before you enrol their help.

Please note that owners of a Reluctant Partner should get on and write their lists regardless. As we've already established, these boys need to understand that you are 100 per cent serious about emigrating and if they don't want to lose you, they're going to have to rethink a few things. Patience and strength...patience and strength!

Once you have your evening set, do not change or cancel it. The only way you're going to get out of your comfortable rut is to actually make some changes. And the only way you're going to do that is to come up with some goals to aim for.

WRITING YOUR WISH LIST

Putting pen to paper and coming up with your Wish List is what life coaches call goal setting.

'Goals are wonderful, because they give you something to aim for,' says resident life coach Lesley Sumner.[2] 'They must be attainable, realistic and always given a time frame in which to be completed. There are a lot of acronyms flying around, but the one that I always like to use is **GROW**:'[3]

G	is the **goal** itself (your **Wish List**)
R	is the **reality** of the situation
O	are the **options** you have
W	is the '**what** next?'

So let's get going (or should I say growing?).

The ultimate goal is obviously emigrating, but breaking things down into a Wish List gives you something a bit more manageable to work with.

Your Wish List can be as long or short as you like. It must include all the things you ideally want out of life, but not in a '1001-things-to-do-before-I-die-naked-bungee-kind-of-way', more a vision of how you would like to live your day-to-day life in the future.

You will need to do some more visualising. Picture yourself living in a new location, with a new job, new friends and new hobbies. What does the picture look like? Where would you like it to be? What do you want to be doing? What changes are you actually after?

If you are writing your Wish List with a partner or family, they must also write their own. And EVERYONE must pay attention to each other's choices! It's all about finding your new routine, cutting out the things you dislike about living in the UK and replacing them with new and exciting things that YNC has to offer.

Being realistic is THE KEY to a good emigration. Whatever you write on your Wish List, it must always remain within the realms of reality. Be very careful not to start writing a Wish List about a new-and-improved 'super you'. The fact that you are about to change the country in which you live does not mean that you can instantly change yourself. Obviously I do not want to be responsible for dashing people's dreams by telling them that they 'can't do this' or 'can't do that', but I would encourage equal measures of enthusiasm and realism. When deciding if you are going to emigrate and where to emigrate to, it's important to remember your boundaries.

Three key boundaries that people need to consider are: language, cash and job skills.

LANGUAGE

If you can't speak Spanish, you're not going to learn through osmosis or by visiting your local Tapas bar. Sad but true and even though the best way to pick up a new language is to throw yourself in at the deep end, not many professional companies will take on a new employee who can only say 'hello', 'thank you' and 'can I order a beer, please?' in the appropriate language.

Studies show that one of the main reasons for people not getting on in their new country is not speaking the lingo! Think about it, it affects every aspect of your life. You can't converse or socialise, you can't navigate local bureaucracy or employment opportunities, you can't perform day-to-day functions without unnecessary agro and, as an end result, you become more isolated from your new fellow countrymen and women. The pitfalls of not being able to make oneself understood (or able to understand others) are plentiful. And with the language uptake at GCSE level dropping by nearly 13 per cent between 2005-2006,[4] the future is not exactly bright for bilingual Brits, so ask yourself the following questions.

- Do you have a basic command of the language already... and we're talking enough to manage on a day-to-day basis?
- How you will earn a living? Do you need to speak the language in order to get a job – or can you get by using English?
- Can you study at evening school before you go and will this realistically make a difference?
- Are you interested in teaching English abroad?
- If you don't already have a basic command of the language, could you blag it?
- ...Are you absolutely sure about that?

Whatever your personal stance on learning a new language, the psychological one should not be ignored either. Many expats would agree that you will settle into a country far quicker and be accepted far more readily if you make the effort to speak the language. Even if you're not very good at it, most locals appreciate it when you at least make an effort to converse in their mother tongue.

CASH
We will look at cash in more detail later, but in the meantime try to be brutally realistic about your financial circumstances – your bank account will undergo a severe battering once you begin the

emigrating process. If all you have is five grand's worth of credit card debt and a £10 Dorothy Perkins gift voucher, you will need to redress the issue of funding your escape!

JOB SKILLS

Be honest with yourself. If you have a background in nursing and have worked in a hospital for the last 15 years, don't assume that you can earn a wage in YNC by rescuing dolphins or becoming the new fashion stylist at Italian *Vogue*. It may sound like a dream job, but you're not really qualified just yet. Yes, have goals, hobbies, become a volunteer, try some work experience or even retrain once you are settled. But bear in mind that it is highly unlikely you will be able earn a decent wage from doing these worthy things as soon as you touch down on Terra Firma.

Write down what you *can do*, as well as what you *would love to have the opportunity to do* in the future. Keep them both in mind, but keep them very separate and who knows, dolphin hugging or fashion styling may come with time!

Finally, one of the most popular job ideas that people write on their Wish Lists and that TV programmes such as *A Place In the Sun* promote is: 'Sell the semi in Basingstoke, give up the office job, live on a small island in the Bora-Bora atoll and open a beach bar – simple!'

Well no, not necessarily. If you didn't do it in the UK, what makes you so sure that you can do it in an unfamiliar foreign country? You're not going to magically develop hospitality management skills on the flight over and starting your own business involves knowledge, experience, contacts and, most importantly, your hard-earned cash!

Lots of people start new businesses when they emigrate, but the question you have to ask yourself is, which people are still successfully running one a year later? The realists – that's who!

Nothing is impossible and, of course, we should all aim for the stars, but at the same time we need to be reasonable and realistic. So do me a favour and keep your feet firmly on the ground.

Keep your **O**ptions open. It's as simple as that.

When you're writing your Wish List, try to be flexible with your thinking. For example, if you are looking for work in YNC and you can't find a job that suits your CV, think a little more 'out of the box'. Look for something that requires similar skills. If you are a dental receptionist, could you become a receptionist for another type of medical practice? If you are an executive PA, could you start off doing some basic secretarial work until you discover your ideal job? Being flexible to start with will help you reach your goals later down the line and thoroughly exploring all of the options open to you in YNC will make all the difference. So think ahead and do your emigrating homework!

And finally: **W**hat next? Keep on reading – that's what!

Rather than my keep telling you what not to do, let's study some Wish List examples to get you in the mood, read through the following statements and select one that most closely represents you (results on page 48).

Wish List: Example One

I WANT TO:
- live in a smarter neighbourhood;
- move to a house with an extra bedroom and a big garden;
- go back to college and retrain as a teacher;
- do a bit more exercise and lose some weight;
- own a pair of Choos;
- have a wedding in Brighton next June;
- have three kids asap;
- teach my partner that there is more to sex than the missionary position;
- learn Kung Fu.

Wish List: Example Two

I WANT TO:
- leave the UK immediately;
- live next to the ocean, under a palm tree;
- work in a beach bar;
- experience as many cultures as is humanly possible;
- work on a sailing boat;
- live by the mountains and go skiing before breakfast;
- work on a kibbutz;
- eat three-minute noodles and not give a damn;
- play snogging games with strangers;
- wear a bikini to work.

Wish List: Example Three	**Wish List: Example Four**
I WANT TO: • move to Brazil even though I can't speak Portuguese; • own a mansion with a heart-shaped swimming pool; • drive a pink Cadillac; • work as a daytime television presenter; • marry Brad Pitt; • grow four inches taller and lose 12 pounds; • have rich friends who take me clothes shopping on a regular basis; • own a pet poodle called Patrick; • learn to fly rocket ships in my spare time.	*I WANT TO:* • move somewhere hot; • live in a quiet town on the south coast of My New Country; • be near the beach; • marry my partner, have three kids and live in a house that can accommodate them; • work as an accountant while training to be a scuba-diving instructor; • learn Pilates/water polo/origami; • stop being such a consumer and live a more environmentally responsible life; • start packing.

ANSWERS

EXAMPLE ONE: THE TWEAKER

You may have been thinking about emigrating, but you don't really, truly want to. You just need to make a few adjustments. Often, when we're a bit disgruntled with life we charge around trying to make huge elaborate changes, when actually all we needed was a tweak. What you thought was a burning ambition to move to another country was simply a desire to change your job, your address, your wardrobe, or even your boyfriend. Wood – trees, you get the picture.

Don't get your decisions mixed up. Tuck this book away somewhere safe – you never know if those tweaks will develop into more of a strong tug!

EXAMPLE TWO: THE BACKPACKER

You are NOT writing an itinerary for your next backpacking trip.

This is NOT meant to be a temporary decision and you are NOT planning a big lovely holiday. If you are interested in seeing the world and experiencing everything there is to experience, go for it! Save up, book your flight and travel the globe until your credit card melts. But be very clear about your priorities here, because emigrating is NOT to be confused with backpacking.

But before you dash off and swap this little book for a *Lonely Planet* guide – remember this. As we've already discussed, a large percentage of people who've emigrated have started small and worked their way up. One minute you've got a rucksack on your back and are marching confidently across a continent, the next you've returned to sign the paperwork and are settling down in YNC. You see, as you're about to find out, backpacking is a bit like catching a raging case of herpes. Once it gets into your system, it cannot be removed and you never know when it will flare up...or develop into a full-blown bout of emigration.

As with Example One, hide this book away for the moment. But don't forget where you put it...because you'll be back!

EXAMPLE THREE: THE DELUSIONAL NUTCASE

Mmm, OK, what part of 'be realistic' don't you understand? Put this book down and go and have a quiet word with yourself.

EXAMPLE FOUR: THE SENSIBLE GIRL

BINGO – you've got your Wish List! You've marked up the goalposts and now have something to aim for. Top of the class, carry on!

THE TOP TEN EMIGRATION DESTINATIONS
FOR SENSIBLE BRITISH GIRLS[5]
...AND WHERE THE BOYS GO TOO!

	The Sensible Girl's Top Ten Emigration Destinations	The Sensible Boy's Top Ten Emigration Destinations
1	AUSTRALIA	AUSTRALIA
2	SPAIN	SPAIN
3	FRANCE	FRANCE
4	NEW ZEALAND	USA
5	USA	NEW ZEALAND
6	GERMANY	CANADA
7	CANADA	GERMANY
8	THAILAND	UAE
9	UNITED ARAB EMIRATES (UAE)	NETHERLANDS
10	NETHERLANDS	SWITZERLAND

CHAPTER 4

NARROWING DOWN YOUR SEARCH

*You've got to be very careful if you don't know where you are going,
because you might not get there.*
LAWRENCE 'YOGI' BERRA[1]

As we've already established, there can be many factors influencing
where a Sensible Person finally decides to settle, which can range
from searching for sunshine to hunting down the bigger pay
cheque. The Top Ten Emigration Destinations list reveals that
Sensible Girls and Guys can sometimes differ on where they
decide to emigrate to (although ideally not if they're going out
with each other at the time) and these differences are quite
revealing.

The emigration ratio between British men and women is pretty even and has remained so since the mid-1970s at around 52:48 (man to woman).[2] And while a quarter of Brits abroad cite 'lifestyle and climate' as being the main reason for their move,[3] others are seeking employment opportunities in countries more associated with economic migration. It seems that 'lifestyle countries' such as Australia, New Zealand and Canada will always be high on our lists, but naturally it's not just our Wish Lists that dictate which country to select. Political and economic stability in YNC will be a major factor when making a decision. A country that was once renowned for offering great career opportunities might now be struggling with unemployment or instability, thus losing its status on the Top Ten Destinations Emigration list. So remember that things can change and that keeping up to speed with your potential new country's 'status' is key.

It's important for you to know that a major reason for British people returning home from an unsuccessful emigration is a lack of preparation and research. For example, studies show that Spain, while being the second most popular emigration destination for Sensible Girls, has one of the highest 'return rates'.[4] In recent times, this can be put down to the Economic Downturn, but one of the other theories behind this phenomenon is that it is considered much easier to emigrate to Spain in the first place (compared to countries like Australia or the US) and therefore people become a little bit more...well...spontaneous with their emigration plans.

I hate to be a party pooper here, but let's get one thing straight.

Being spontaneous is essential in the bedroom.

Being spontaneous is great when booking a last-minute romantic weekend break to Prague.

However, being spontaneous in the planning (or should I say *lack* of planning) of your emigration is not sensible at all and will probably result in the repacking of one's bags shortly after arrival and returning to the UK with a face like a slapped arse.

Do YOU want to have a face like a slapped arse?

No...thought not.

To avoid stuffing up your emigration, you need to thoroughly research YNC, although maybe we should start referring to it as Your New Town or City,* as we really need to start narrowing things down a bit.

The Internet, books, TV programmes and Wish Lists will all help to establish exactly *where* that special place might be, but most Sensible Girls usually have a pretty good idea of where they are aiming for from the start. They just need to do a bit of fine-tuning. It's stating the obvious, but try not to generalise in your

---

* Or village/hamlet/field in the middle of nowhere...

decision-making. Spain isn't all beaches and sangria; Barcelona isn't just a city full of fancy architecture, and so on. You need to get specific with locations and really focus on whether these places have what's required for you to build a new life – indefinitely. Think of your research as one giant-Google-Earth-search, zoning and zooming in on potential settling-down-spots.

Generally speaking, a couple of 'jollies' abroad will not give you a firm enough basis for uprooting your life and plonking it down on foreign shores. Sensible Girls know that only a Club 18–30 holiday rep would consider emigrating to Cyprus, based on a drug-fuelled snogfest in Ayia Napa. It is all about making intelligent and informed choices.

Holidays may have planted a little seed in your brain about one day going to live there, but you must do a bit more homework in order to pass your emigrating exams. You may know where to dance the night away or buy fabulous sparkly flip-flops, but that's not going to help you find your new routine. You need to see the areas where you are considering moving to, with a view to moving there – if you see what I mean. In other words, you don't just need a holiday; you need to do some reconnaissance.

THE RECCE

Obviously I'm not suggesting that you need to undertake military-style visits on a bi-weekly basis, but you do need to try to make at least one decent recce trip to look at things with a fresh, non-touristy pair of eyes. You are deciding if you would like to move 'over there' indefinitely and whether you like everything as much as you thought you did when on holiday. You are not just looking for somewhere to sunbathe and party (although that can be part of the equation). You are looking for a place to live, work and play – a place to call home.

As we've already discussed, one of the main rules of emigration is being realistic and this recce will be no exception to the rule. Sensible Girls can, at times, become highly excitable. And unfortunately one of these 'excitable times' is when undertaking a recce to their new country. There's something in the air, a tang of anticipation, an undeniable whiff of excitement and, after a couple of lungs-full, Sensible Girls run the risk of losing any sense of reality they had. Once 'away with the emigrating fairies', strange conversations ensue (alternatively known as 'talking bollocks') and even the fairies start wondering what on earth's going on.

In order to avoid talking twaddle, I have picked out a few classic statements that are to be avoided at all costs. If you (or indeed anyone in your emigrating party) utter any of the following while on your recce – a good, firm slap is probably required.

'Oh look...I quite fancy doing that'
Any recce must be undertaken minus your rose-tinted holiday sunglasses – the ones you drunkenly wore when you and your girlfriends sat in that dodgy beach bar and said: 'Gosh, why don't we all get jobs here.' If you are emigrating (rather than backpacking) you need to find a decent job in YNC – so be sensible.

'Oooh...let's renovate that old chicken shed and open a B&B'
Brits are obsessed both with renovating and with B&Bs. But this deadly combination costs money and is tough to start with. Yep, lots of people have done it, and you can do it too, but don't think that you will be making a couple of fry-ups each morning in your luxurious newly converted bird coop and then heading off to the beach. This option is not an alternative to hard work; it *is* hard work!

'Mmm, it's so peaceful here'
Well, it would be because you've only experienced it in 'holiday mode' before. You're either in bed nursing a hangover or barbequing yourself on the beach, so you're not exactly exposing yourself to the raised volume levels of a typical rush hour.

Rather than having a 'lie in' on this recce, get up and have a go at commuting. Who cares if you don't have a job to go to? Leave your holiday hire car behind and jump on some form of public transport, then see what really happens.

'Arrrrr, the locals are super-friendly, bless 'em'
Tour guides, scuba instructors, barmen – these people don't really count. You're paying them, so they're bound to be friendly to you. What you need is a good, strong dose of genuine local life.

Go and find some non-touristy shops. The Twinkly Sparkly Flip-Flop Emporium next to your hotel does not count. Get out there and thoroughly explore the areas which you are thinking of moving to. Do a spot of food shopping, check out the supermarkets, grab some lunch in the centre of town, find the local drinking establishment and have the foreign equivalent of a swift half. These everyday tasks will give you a much clearer idea of what life is really like, rather than lazing by the pool all afternoon.

'Flipping heck – we can afford a mansion out here'
Can you really?

Or are you looking at what your current UK wage can afford? By the time you've paid off your debts, paid for your emigration, found a job and started earning YNC's wage, are we still talking mansion...or maisonette?

'Gosh, I can't wait to live by the beach!'
Neither can the other 98.5 per cent of the population.

Don't be fooled into thinking that you can march into YNC and instantly afford the dream house by the sea. You may find that you have to work towards this real estate goal.

As we all know, if you want to live in a 'room with a view', you will have to pay for the privilege. It's the same in any country, so talk to some estate agents, find the property section in local papers and look at the kind of places you can afford. Are they even within a sniff of the ocean or would you be living in a high-rise block in the suburbs which looks suspiciously similar to the one in which you're living now?

'Do you speaky thee engleesh?'
Yeeees – I don't think we need to dwell on this one. Just do your fellow expats a favour and try NOT to embarrass us!

'It's always sunny and hot here'
Well it might not be...how do you know?

Unless you're moving to the desert or relocating to somewhere in the tropics, YNC will have some kind of seasonal variation to its climate. The chances are you have always visited during the fairer summer months. What is it like in winter? Will that eternal sunshine you've been dreaming about be washed away by monsoonal rains every year? Will you need to pack a hot-water bottle and thermal undies?

The weather can affect other factors as well. If the place to which you are thinking of moving relies heavily on tourism, is it possible to have a snoop around during high *and* low seasons? Some places practically shut down during low season while others will be overwhelmed by tourists during peak times, making things quite frenetic. So it's handy to know whether you'll be living in a bustling tourist mecca one month, which turns into a ghost town the next.

'But I love the countryside; I would never get bored'
You've put those pink specs on again haven't you? It's all very picturesque, but what happens when you've finished admiring that view?

If you've lived in a city most of your life and list your hobbies as window shopping and binge drinking, you will probably need a bit of civilisation on your doorstep. Would you consider moving to the highlands of Scotland or to an isolated farm in Wales? No? Well, why are you looking at this property in the middle of nowhere then?

Try not to be dazzled by the fact that you can afford a property with a vineyard and olive grove (unless you are a dab hand at viticulture or olive oil production) and get real. You need to work. You need to make new friends. You need to be near somewhere that serves a decent latte and you don't want to go stir crazy after two months of living in a field!

Some people, whose emigration is part of a career overhaul, might not have the luxury of choosing where they emigrate to. Instead they will be heading off to where the job takes them. But that doesn't mean to say that a recce isn't required. A poke around YNC before you actually have to knuckle down and start work is a good way of acclimatising and preparing yourself for life abroad. So try to get out there to have a squizz.

Whether you have selected somewhere in the South of France where you holidayed as a little girl or a fabulous spot in Vancouver where you worked during your backpacking years, you should have narrowed things down to specific areas by now. So why waste any more time umming and aahhing about whether you want to go? Of course you do, otherwise your brain wouldn't keep nagging you when you're not concentrating properly.

OK, so now that you have worked out WHO you are, WHAT you want and WHERE you think you can find it...we can take another step forward and work out HOW you're going to achieve it! And that's one of the most exciting steps yet, because you're about to come up with your Master Plan!

CHAPTER 5

THE MASTER PLAN

On the keyboard of life, always keep one finger on the escape key.
SCOTT ADAMS[1]

It's a well-known fact that us girls are much better at organising ourselves (and other people) than the boys. Hence the reason for this book not being called *The Sensible Boy's Guide to Emigrating Brilliantly.** If it were, UK emigration figures would plummet and the line of Brits queuing to leave the country would miraculously find itself winding its way down to the nearest boozer.

---

* Although I suppose I could have called it *The Slightly Useless Boy's Guide to Getting Your Arse Off The Sofa and Helping Your Girlfriend Emigrate*...but it wasn't really catchy enough!

There are many differences between how men and women undertake and experience emigration and Mark Chapman, series producer of the *A Place In...* TV programmes has had a front-row seat and been able observe quite a few of them:[2]

'Without doubt, the women have thought through their move much better than the men. The women have worked through the emotional wrench of leaving their family, friends and the UK lifestyle.

'The men are far less sorted. They like the idea of making a big dramatic step, but they have rarely considered the true impact of such a move. They enjoy the hunt for new property, the logistics of travel, etc., but inevitably have cold feet once they are actually about to make the break. They feel insecure, often realising for the first time that their partner may be relying on them to lead the way in a foreign environment, where they (often) don't speak the language and don't really understand the culture.'

Our resident expat coaches Sabina and Nynke[3] also observe differences between the way boys and girls deal with emigration:

'We experience that women need more encouragement as they tend to give priority to their partner's or children's needs. We observe that when women are taken away from their comfort zone, leaving family, friends and a career behind, they *are* still able to adapt to their new country.'

And once Sensible Girls move overseas, Sabina and Nynke have spotted what could be described as an inner strength evolving:

'We see women that stand up for themselves, who are happy and very proud of themselves. They feel that they are moving forward in a way they wouldn't have done if they had stayed at home.'[4]

So, you see, it is up to us girls to mastermind moving abroad. You could even say that from now on WE will be wearing the trousers. And that is why it is going to be up to YOU to construct and carry out your Master Plan.

As we've already established, the key to implementing a good Master Plan is making it realistic. It needs to be do-able. You need to take small, manageable bite-sized pieces out of that emigration pie rather than trying to shove the whole thing down your throat in one go – and gagging on it.

So, we will break the planning down into chewable chunks. To start off with, you are going to need the following organisational tools:

1. THE INTERNET

This will be the most indispensable tool you will use.

Google the word 'emigrate' and see how websites are out there. Far more than any Sensible Girl will get through, that's for sure. And while there is no doubt that there are plenty of websites to guide you through the emigration process, the trick is finding ones that are both reliable and appropriate to your personal circumstances.

Bureaucratic rules and regulations, financial advice, property markets, travel requirements – in fact all of the key components of your emigration – have an annoying habit of changing unexpectedly, especially in the current global financial market. So, with communications being as speedy as they now are, printed information can be well past its expiry date before you know it.

Your mission is to be able to differentiate between the helpful emigration websites and the unhelpful ones, because if you get the two confused it could get messy.

While researching this book, it was impossible to avoid the large number of rather useless emigration websites out there. If some are to be believed, we can all rush out and buy our air tickets tomorrow morning and head off to our very own piece of tropical real estate. Do yourself a favour, avoid time-wasters and trust your own research.

You can start with UK government websites, YNC's official embassy and immigration websites and recommended immigration and relocation agents. You can read emigration blogs or pages of 'top tips' and 'handy hints' on expat forums. There are hundreds of chat rooms, where Brits abroad have cyber chats on everything from Visa points to where they can find a bag of Wotsits. Sure – you are entering into unknown territory (literally), but it really shouldn't take too long to differentiate between bona fide information providers and scam artists who charge for some dubiously researched information that you could probably have Googled in 20 seconds or less.

You know where you want to go. You know what you're looking for (well almost). So DON'T doubt your own decision-making abilities and DO be discerning when spending your money on emigration service providers.

On a more practical level, if you don't have a computer with broadband Internet access at home, take every available opportunity to do your research at work during quiet times. A home PC may give you privacy, but an office one gives you full use of...well...the office. Not only a trusty computer, but a fax, phone and more stationery than you can shake a Pritt Stick at. Just take care your boss doesn't notice, otherwise you may find yourself leaving a bit earlier than you had originally intended.

2. CALENDAR

It doesn't matter whether it's an homage to Hogwarts or George Clooney, so long as the calendar gives you enough space to write things down clearly, it's good enough for the job.

Keep a record of ANYTHING you have planned towards emigrating, even if it's retrospectively logging something you've just done. This will mean that you can always refer back to your calendar if there's a problem.

In the next few months you are going to be like a Spandex-clad plate-spinner from one of those rubbish 70s' variety shows. You will have a huge amount of projects on the go, all at the same time and you must keep a watchful eye on everything. You will find that some people are helpful and others require a gentle reminder, nudge or smack, so it is always good to know exactly where you stand in the proceedings and a well-documented calendar is the perfect solution.

3. CALCULATOR

There's no magic formula and there's no specific amount of cash that will guarantee you a smooth transition into your foreign future. Basic maths applies here. If you don't do your sums properly, you won't be able to afford to emigrate.

4. LISTS

As you can tell from this book – I'm a BIG fan of list making!

Keep religiously making lists, otherwise you are going to come a cropper with your plate-spinning exercises. Lists have become your new best friend: look after them, give them plenty of attention, buy them roses and expensive chocolates, but don't ignore them or they'll trip you up and poke you in the eye.

5. A GOOD OLD-FASHIONED ADDRESS BOOK

You know where all your friends live, but you don't know their postcodes.

You have your friends' phone numbers, but they're saved on your UK mobile.

You have everyone's e-mail address, but only on your work PC, home laptop or BlackBerry®.

What you need is an old-fashioned, 'no batteries required' Little Black Book that won't lose all the valuable information if it gets dropped.

6. A GOOD OLD-FASHIONED BIRTHDAY BOOK

It's not going to be easy remembering your Aunty Dotty's 95th birthday or sister's wedding anniversary, especially if you're about to embark on a teaching course in the middle of South America. So find a birthday book (small monthly, non-year-specific calendar) in which you can list all important dates, birthdays, anniversaries, etc. Even dates that you take for granted like Mother's or Father's days can fall on completely different dates overseas, so write everything down now and you'll be thankful (and popular) later. After all, you can't expect people to remember your birthday if you can't be bothered to remember theirs.

7. A LARGE BOX CONCERTINA FILE

This will be where all your UK paperwork is stored. It's going to be so beautifully organised that the trustworthy person you will eventually leave it with (your Box Guardian) will be able to pull out your bank statements, exam certificates or tax returns in the blink of an eye. It will be neatly labelled, contain only essential paperwork and be kept somewhere easily accessible by the trustworthy custodian.

The chances are you won't need much from this file once you've left the UK. But if you do, all it will take is a quick scan and e-mail. In the meantime, everything is stashed away safe and sound and you do not have to worry about an extra piece of luggage in an alarmingly growing pile.

Once you are settled and have a permanent base, you can decide whether or not to bring it out. You may find that everything has become slightly irrelevant by then, but at least whenever you return to the UK, everything is where you left it.

8. USB

Even if you're carrying a laptop in your hand luggage, you want to make sure that all important documents, work files, contacts and emigration paperwork are saved somewhere safe, accessible (and easy to carry). A USB can fit in your handbag which means you know that if all else fails, you can plug it in and get what you need. So you always have back-up.

9. EAR MUFFS†

Once people begin to discover your escape plan, some will feel the urge to point out that you are stark raving mad (most will think you're fantastic – but there's always someone who feels the need to 'p**s on your chips'). These grouches could be anyone from work colleagues, friends or even family. So if the going gets tough and you've had enough of their opinions...

10. ALCOHOL

OK, without wishing to sound like a raging lush, beer and wine can indeed help with emigration angst.

Because sometimes you will feel like the whole idea of emigrating is totally and utterly ridiculous. 'What *were* you thinking?'. 'Surely it's far more sensible to go shopping and forget about it.' You will have blazing rows with your partner about whether you want to sell the UK property or rent it out, whether you pack your DVDs or his CD collection, but whatever the problem, don't give up.

Stop everything.

Pour yourself a decent glass of wine.

---

† Ear muffs are not a legitimate fashion accessory and should under no circumstances be worn in public.

And take a break.

11. COUNTRY-SPECIFIC EMIGRATING BOOK

Yes...I know you've bought this one. But this is the book before the book. What I mean is this book is the *amuse bouche* of emigrating literature: it sort of gets you in the mood before the main meal arrives.

Even though emigration books can become out of date relatively quickly, the principles behind their statistics don't, so there is a lot to be said for nipping out and purchasing a trusty old emigrating bible on YNC and doing a bit of bedtime reading to get you in the mood. From now on we will refer to your Country-Specific Emigrating book as your CSE Book.

12. BILINGUAL DICTIONARY/FOREIGN PHRASE BOOK

We've already established the necessity for Sensible Girls to try to speak the lingo in their new country so a decent phrase book provides a good starting block for doing so. Plus, if you are seen to be making an effort – people will be far more smiley and helpful.

Once you have gone out and purchased some or all of the above, you are ready for the next step.

We will be starting with a chapter called 'The paperwork', which is about finding your way in legally. This is a big chapter and stands alone. The reason for this is very simple. If you don't have the points or the paperwork to get into YNC, you're not going anywhere. So you need to tick that one off of your list before you go any further.

But once you're through – we can look at **planning your future** and **managing your past**. Then, it's a hop, skip and a jump over to YNC for the final section of the book, which will focus on **settling down**. These three manageable portions will be divided into various categories and will look something like this:

YOUR EMIGRATING MASTER PLAN

1. Future planning	2. Past management	3. Current co-ordination

Planting seeds All the preparation you need to do, so that you (plus partner, family, belongings and whatever else you wish to take with you) can get to YNC sensibly, safely, legally, happily and with a good chance of making things work.	**Tying up loose ends** All the preparation you have to do in the UK in order to organise your life to a point that you can leave it neatly and indefinitely behind.	**Settling in** Everything you need to think of to kick-start your brand new foreign life into action, so that you feel happy and settled in your new home.
UK-based organisation *(before emigrating)*	**UK-based organisation** *(before emigrating)*	**YNC-based organisation** *(after emigrating)*

Be warned that the UK-based organisations will start overlapping and running simultaneously so that you will be tying up loose ends and planting seeds all at the same time. But Sensible Girls are great at multitasking and full of common sense, so prioritising should not be a problem.

While this book is written in a particular order, your emigration might not follow suit, so don't worry if you get stuck on a particular topic. Just keep crossing things off your 'to do lists' and chant the following mantra three times a day:

'I AM AN ELEGANT ESCAPE ARTIST WHO WILL EMIGRATE EASILY.'

OK, is your seatbelt securely fastened? Are you holding on tight? Scream if you want to go faster!

CHAPTER 6

THE PAPERWORK

Multitasking is the ability to screw everything up simultaneously.
JEREMY CLARKSON[1]

> **The Golden Rule of Emigrating**
> If you are not 100 per cent sure about the
> legalities of living and working in your
> chosen country, research them
> meticulously until you are!

Obtaining the correct paperwork in order to successfully emigrate is a tricky process, and depending on the individual's circumstances (and choice of country) can vary significantly in complexity. After all, there are a lot of Sensible Girls out there and a lot of countries to choose from, so attempting to cater for everyone would be like trying to squeeze an elephant into a pair of Louboutins. Aside from needing a book the size of *War and Peace* to accommodate the information, it would also need to be updated every five minutes, as immigration policies have a nasty habit of changing.

The most sensible place to get started when doing your research is with YNC's Department of Immigration website (or equivalent). But be warned: some of them can be pretty heavy going (similar to wading through a tax return). If form filling, question deciphering, point calculating and self-assessment questionnaires fill you with horror, you might want to pour yourself a chilled glass of something alcoholic before logging on. But once you get used to all the acronyms and immigration jargon, you'll get a 'feel' for which routes might be appropriate for you and then be able to start broadening your research.

In many ways, Sensible Girls who are heading for Europe are the lucky ones, because being a UK Citizen instantly grants you the right to work and live in Your New European Country. And while there will still be a certain amount of paperwork required to move to YNEC, it's not half as daunting as some of the more distant country's requirements...but more about them later.

EUROPE

As you've already seen, four out of the top ten emigration destinations chosen by Sensible Girls are in Europe. It's a popular choice and for a good reason: UK nationals have the right to live in any European Economic Area (EEA) country. The EEA is made up of countries that are full members of the European Union (EU), together with Iceland, Liechtenstein and Norway.

At the time of writing[*], there are 27 countries in the European Union (EU):

Austria	Germany	Netherlands
Belgium	Greece	Poland
Bulgaria	Hungary	Portugal

---

[*] This will no doubt change at some point soon.

Cyprus	Republic of Ireland	Romania
Czech Republic	Italy	Slovakia
Denmark	Latvia	Slovenia
Estonia	Lithuania	Spain
Finland	Luxembourg	Sweden
France	Malta	United Kingdom

The European Union collectively has a population of almost half a billion and these figures will probably rise again if (or when) countries like Croatia, the Former Yugoslav Republic of Macedonia and Turkey (all candidate countries) get to join the party.[2]

You may have noticed that Switzerland hasn't been mentioned, as it isn't a member of either the EEA or EU. Fear not, as the land of yodelling does have an agreement with the EU which means that its rules and regulations are similar to theirs.

As a fully-fledged member of the EEA, you have the right to work in any other member country[3] and will be granted the same rights as YNC's nationals when it comes to such things as working conditions, pay, social security matters etc. Countries outside the EU (including the candidate countries we've already discussed) have their own individual rules and regulations, so you'll need to contact their embassy to find out what's what. And if the going gets tough, just count yourself lucky: things can get a lot more complicated once you start looking further afield...

FURTHER AFIELD (TECHNICALLY KNOWN AS THE REST OF THE WORLD)

Governments have always kept a close eye on the flow of people moving in and out of their countries but when something as dramatic as the global financial crisis (GFC) comes along, the delicate relationship between immigrants and the economy comes under even more intense scrutiny. Eight out of the top ten Sensible Countries are members of the Organisation of Economic Co-operation and Development (OECD), who recently predicted that the economic crisis would cause 'the first major fall in the number of migrants coming to work in OECD countries since the 1980s'. But before we all start panicking that immigration departments have gone into lock-down and barricaded themselves in, let's get a bit of perspective. The OECD *also* recommends that countries should 'keep doors open to migrant workers', in order to meet 'long-term labour needs'.[4] In layman's terms, this means fine-tuning their visa requirements, adjusting job lists and making sure that immigration programmes are more effective and demand driven. Which is perfectly sensible, as they can't afford to have every Tom, Dick and Harriet charging in. Think of emigration as being an exclusive party that you're trying to get into. The harder it is to gain entry, the better the party and it's 'invite only' rather than 'tickets on the door'!

While Europe is a popular emigration destination for Sensible Girls, the 'Fantastic Four' feature strongly in the Top Ten:

THE FANTASTIC FOUR†

1. **Australia**
2. **New Zealand**
3. **America**
4. **Canada**

These countries dominate the British emigration landscape and are firm favourites with Sensible Girls not just from the UK but across the globe. There are a wide range of reasons for their popularity; but lifestyle, climate and the fact that they speak English usually swings it for the Brits. The other prime reason for their popularity is the economic one, as they all have a steady demand for skilled migrants. Which brings us neatly onto the topic of visas. Speak to any Sensible Girl who is about to emigrate to one of the Fantastic Four and sooner or later the conversation will veer towards talk of their visa application. So let's start with the Number One country of choice, and go from there.

AUSTRALIA

The Australian immigration system is renowned for its General Skilled Migration (GSM) visas and its infamous 'points' requirements. When deciding what visa option is best for you, one of the first things you will need to do is check whether your occupation is included on their list of jobs in short supply. This is more formally known as the Migration Occupations Demand List or MODL (be warned, it's acronym-tastic in this chapter!).

---

† Up until quite recently, it was The Fantastic Five, as South Africa was proving popular. However after various political and economical 'issues' the country's popularity has waned and immigration figures have dropped as a result. You see? What did I say about change?

The MODL is updated twice a year and covers a broad range of jobs, spanning both blue and white collar career paths[5]. The only problem for Australia was that the applicants weren't evenly distributed across this list. In fact in just three years, the programme delivered 28,800 accountants, 6,500 cooks and 2,800 hairdressers (the mind boggles). Bearing in mind that Australia was suffering a severe shortage of tradesmen during this period, this same programme managed to cough up only 800 bricklayers and 300 carpenters. Or to put it another way, five occupations on the list accounted for almost half the visas granted.[6]

As if that weren't cause enough for Aussie immigration officers to start getting twitchy, along came the horror that is the GFC and things started going down the plughole all over the world. And although it must be noted that Australian unemployment figures rose much slower than a lot of other countries' (and they are still technically not in a recession), Aussies still had to be given first dibs at the job market (rather than Jenny Foreigners), which mean things needed tweaking.

The Skilled Migration Program was re-evaluated and focussed on jobs that were *really* in demand. In March 2009, a different list of jobs called the Critical Skills List (CSL) was drafted, which was much shorter and more specialised. At the time of writing, any GSM application submitted that did not include a job on this CSL list was not being being processed.[7] It's very likely that this state of affairs will change again as soon as the GFC eases off, but it's a clear illustration of how the goalposts can move. So you need to check things on a regular basis.

Along with the CSL, the Australian Department of Immigration announced other changes to their policies back in January 2009. While the Skilled Independent Visa is one of the most popular, priority is now being given to other types of visas such as the Regional Sponsored Migration Scheme and the Employer

Nomination Scheme[8] under the premise that it's far better to offer a visa to someone who's got work lined up already, or who can relocate to a specific regional area where there is a skills (or even a people) shortage! If you're cashed-up or a high-flying business woman, there are business and investment options and likewise, if you have a relative or partner who is an Australian citizen (or permanent resident) you can have a crack at a Family Visa, although don't think this is a done deal, as you will still need to jump through a few hoops.

There are all sorts of variations to these visas, but I think you get the gist and that's probably enough to keep you going. For more information, visit the Australian Department of Immigration and Citizenship's website at **www.immi.gov.au**.

NEW ZEALAND

According to a recent survey[9], 32 per cent of new arrivals to New Zealand emigrated from the UK[10] so it's another popular choice with the Brits and with 52 per cent of all migrants being female; it seems the Land of the Long White Cloud is a real hit with Sensible Girls. As with all of the Fantastic Four, the Skilled Migration route is most popular, with 58 per cent of successful migrants using this method of entry.

Similarly to their Antipodean neighbours, the Kiwis are experiencing a few difficulties as a result of the GFC and by July 2009, New Zealand unemployment had reached a six year high of five per cent.[11] With preference being given to Skilled Visa applicants who either already have a job offer from a NZ employer or are planning on relocating to an area with a skills shortage, this might make things a bit 'tight' for new applications over the coming months, especially as NZ has recently removed 44 occupations from their Immediate Skill Shortage List (ISSL). Stories in the British press have been painting a rather gloomy picture of how tough things have become for Brits who have recently emigrated to NZ but at the same time there are still reports of desperate employers who are crying out for skilled staff. At the time of writing, nurses, social workers, engineers, motor mechanics and a few other professions were listed as being in 'high demand' in New Zealand.[12] And the good news is that applicants who fill these jobs may actually have their applications processed more quickly than usual. So there's always a silver lining – somewhere!

Another change currently taking place within Kiwi Immigration HQ is one that should help protect Sensible Girls who employ the services of an immigration agent. Any application submitted through an unlicensed agent by May 2010 will not be processed (and the same principle began in May 2009 for applications submitted by onshore NZ-based agents).[13] This is a perfectly sensible rule when you consider that around 20,000 skilled Brits emigrated to New Zealand in 2008,[14] some of whom will have employed the services of such an agent...but more of them later.

According to the aforementioned NZ survey, 93 per cent of migrants reported that they were satisfied, or very satisfied, with life in New Zealand, with 'climate' and 'natural beauty' topping the list of things migrants loved most.[15] Working out how to enjoy that scenery and fresh air might take a while but as with Australia, New Zealand has other visa categories aside from the popular Skilled Migrant options, such as Business, Investment and Family Visas, all of which are listed on the New Zealand immigration website (**www.immigration.govt.nz**).

UNITED STATES

According to recent statistics from the US Census Bureau, the American population currently stands at over 305 million, but this figure is definitely on the rise as it's estimated that one immigrant arrives in the US *every 36 seconds*.[16] Imagine the paperwork! The Department of Homeland Security (DHS) is in charge of US immigration, with a branch called the United States Citizenship and Immigration Services (USCIS) monitoring the number of visas issued. With such a huge number of people arriving each year, the US immigration is big and guess what, there are changes on the US Immigration horizon too – good ones!

President Obama has already acknowledged that reform is needed within the immigration departments, and while we are still unclear as to exactly what changes will take place, it's all about improving systems. By the time this book goes to print the USCIS website should have been given a facelift allowing applicants to get updates on the status of their applications,[17] so again, the more you log on, the more up-to-date you will be.

US visas primarily come under two main headings: Temporary Visas (classed as non-immigrant) and Permanent Visas (classed as immigrant). Temporary Visas are the most common route into the US and there are a lot to choose from.

Out of the non-immigrant list, the H-1B is ideal for Sensible Girls who wish to live and work in the US. Selection criteria are based around education and experience and the applicant will be required to secure employment (either full or part-time – which is handy to keep in mind). Unlike Australia and New Zealand, the word 'sponsorship' should not be used when trying to pin down a US employer (who will be required to submit a 'petition') as they're not familiar with the term and might feel that you're trying to dupe them.[18] Instead, just focus on securing a job offer and tell potential employers that you 'will be granted permission to work exclusively for them', once you've submitted the paperwork. This makes you sound like less of a liability.

As with all the other countries, there are plenty of other visa options available. The EB-3 is a popular permanent visa (again, for skilled professional workers). Another area expected to change is that relating to the Family Visa categories. With America still in the grip of a recession, this would be a far less controversial one to upgrade, as it's not viewed as actively taking jobs away from US citizens, so with changes around the corner this may be a way of gaining a smoother ride into YNC (or indeed NYC!). Again, there are also Business Visas, Intra-Company Visas (which, if you work for a company that has an office in America, means you might be able to get a transfer) and many, many more.

The USCIS website is **www.uscis.gov**, and while there are a myriad of other sites that will help you in your quest, you'd be wise to start off here.

CANADA

Canada enjoys a very positive relationship with immigration and this is reflected in its population: one in six residents were born outside the country.[19] As with Australia and New Zealand, the skilled visa is the most popular category, accounting for approximately 60 per cent of the country's immigrant intake.[20]

Canadian Federal Skilled Worker Applications, just like their Antipodean equivalents, have a few pre-requisites. Sensible Girls are required to either have an offer of employment or be a foreign national living legally in Canada for a year (as either a foreign worker or international student), or be a skilled worker who has at least one year's experience in one or more of the occupations listed on the National Occupational Classification List (NOCL). (They all love their lists, don't they!)[21]

The latter option is by far the most popular but according to experts[22] this list of 38 occupations is likely to (you've guessed it) change. At the time of writing, nothing had been posted on the official website, but that's not to say these changes won't have taken place by the time you have your hands on this book! As with Australia and New Zealand, it all depends on how the world economic dramas pan out in the months ahead.

Unlike the other top five countries, Canada has two official languages – English and French. 60 per cent of people speak English, 23 per cent speak French and 85 per cent of those French-speaking Canadians live in Quebec.[23] Which incidentally has its own immigration requirements and selects candidates independently from the rest of the country (this could be a sensible route in for you if you can speak French). Another popular route into the country is via the Provincial Nominee Program. All options have separate selection criteria and are designed to give Canada's provinces more control over the movement of immigrants into their patch. This route has similar merits to the Australian Regional Sponsored Migration Scheme, in that it encourages a better spread of immigrants across the country (rather than everyone huddling around the key cities) which will in turn address skills shortages on a province by province basis. And, if you're an applicant with skills that are currently in demand, you could find your application fast-tracked, so again it's not all bad news!

As with the other four, there are the other options such as Business and Investor Visas as well as Family Class Visas. Citizenship and Immigration Canada's official website is packed with all the immigration options, so log onto **www.cic.gc.ca** and swot up.

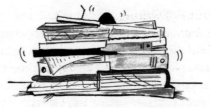

Are you still with me? It is a bit technical, I know, but basically, depending on the country of choice, there are lots and lots of different routes in, and it's very much a case of selecting the one that is absolutely right for you. Here are a few more general points to consider when investigating your paperwork.

Start your research off with YNC's official immigration website (as listed) along with the hundreds of other websites dedicated to YNC/moving overseas (**www.visabureau.com** is a good one to kick-off with) and before you know it, you'll find yourself making some informed decisions about what the best policy is for your application. Your trusty CSE book can also help as can UK emigration publications such as *Emigrate*↗ Magazine. The most important thing here is that you get the bureaucratic ball rolling as soon as you can. While EEA/EU countries will need less paperwork, others (as you're starting to learn) require *reams* and the process can take months or even years. When you've decided which visa (or equivalent) to apply for, make sure you have everything ready before you lodge the application, as once that ball starts rolling, you don't want it to stop because you forgot something. And in the meantime, don't make any irreversible decisions until you are absolutely sure your application will be accepted. Patience is the key here.

OTHER PAPERWORK

You may be required to present various types of ID and documentation. Dig everything out and if you are required to mail stuff, send copies wherever possible.[‡] Always scan and save everything that you send off, for instant back-up. When filling out a form, make sure you've included all the necessary information to avoid unnecessary delays

Chances are, you will be required to get hold of a police clearance form, which should take ten working days[24] (excluding days of receipt and dispatch), so pay a visit to your local cop shop and lodge your application with the rozzers as soon as you can. Also bear in mind that embassies/high commissions usually require the form to be less than six months old. So if your application has taken longer, you might need to go back and ask for another one (which is technically referred to as a 'pain in the arse'). The same principle goes for medicals, which may need to be re-done if paperwork isn't stamped in time.

If you are applying for a visa that will eventually be stuck in your passport, double-check when your current passport runs out. It will be very irritating if, once you get your precious visa, your passport expires shortly afterwards and you have to faff around getting things reissued. Your passport does not need to have expired in order for you to apply for another one, just have a chat with the friendly people at the Post Office as they should be able to advise you. And obviously...keep an eye on dates and do not leave applying until the very last minute, as that's only going to add to the stress load.

[‡] Some of your more important documents will need to have 'certified copies' taken. This simply means they need to be photocopied and signed by lawyer (or suchlike) who is essentially confirming that you're not getting the Tippex out and making a few little amendments!

IMMIGRATION AGENCIES

Immigration agencies are *very* popular. The chances are YNC has accredited immigration agencies; there should be a list of reputable ones recommended on YNC's government or embassy websites. While Sensible Girls can usually manage on their own, it can be worth paying for their services in the long run. They will help you through the piles of paperwork and can give you a better understanding of how the system works.

Most emigration specialist websites have online evaluation questionnaires that act as a good indicator as to whether your application will be successful or not. Once you've had a fiddle around on the website, you will be ready to talk to a human being.

Your initial consultation should be free and should give you a realistic idea of whether or not you are likely to be granted a particular visa. If the agency is a reputable one, it will be honest about your chances (rather than taking your money and stringing you along). Try to meet with a consultant face-to-face rather than dealing with them via the phone or Internet. Even if the agency doesn't have a UK-based consultant, it will often have representatives who visit Britain on a regular basis.

Don't be shy about querying the agent's qualifications and references before committing to anything, either. A registered agent gives you added security, as they are bound by a code of conduct that makes them answerable to professional immigration bodies. Depending on the country you are emigrating to, there will often be an immigration governing organisation that they need to be members of and who makes sure they behave themselves (remember New Zealand's licensing rules!). So check if they're 'in the club'. Do not hand over a single penny until you understand what it is they are going to do for you and you are completely happy and comfortable with everything. And don't forget that just because you 'go' with an agent, it doesn't guarantee that you'll get the visa or residency paperwork you want; but it should make the process a lot simpler, though.

OPTIONS

Be prepared to be flexible as you might not be able to secure a gold-plated citizenship to YNC in one fell swoop, especially after the GFC. Governments often prefer to control their immigration rates and overcome skills shortages by simply granting one- or two-year renewable visas, which means you may have to spend a few years in limbo before you build up to that dual citizenship you've always dreamt of.

If you find that gaining entry to your chosen country is looking shaky, never forget that there is always more than one way to skin a cat. Make sure that you have explored all your options. For example, you might not have enough points to become a 'skilled migrant' and move to Australia, but if you find a company that's willing to sponsor you, you may be able to get a different type of visa. Likewise, you might need to compromise on your emigration destination and move away from the big city...as regional visas are often more accommodating, and more speedily processed (if you're lucky!).

Emigrating can be a gamble – literally. If you want to move to the US, there is the unusual option of entering 'The Green Card Lottery', otherwise known as the Diversity Immigrant Visa Program. This system arranges for 55,000 people to be granted the chance to apply for permanent residency in the US. Forms can be found on the official Government website,[25] but hold your horses – unless you are a Sensible Girl from Northern Ireland, you won't be allowed to 'play' as the rest of the United Kingdom maxes out their immigration quota and is therefore exempt.

We have already established that systems change. What was once required for entry into a particular country may suddenly be up- or down-graded. New countries may be granted membership to the EU or governments may decide they have a shortage of skilled workers and all of a sudden your once insufficient credentials become ample. Likewise, the changes can swing against you and the points you have might no longer be enough.

Depending on your circumstances, another back-door approach into YNC can be via the student entrance. As with everything else, the rules vary from country to country, but if you are running out of options, it is a good idea to research the benefits of revisiting the classroom. Just make sure you think ahead when using further education as a stepping stone into YNC, as some countries are more likely than others, to offer permanent residency as a bi-product!

If you fancy yourself as an entrepreneur, there may well be a specific visa for you. Governments like the idea of people bringing money into their country to create employment. There may even be new business schemes waiting for you on 'the other side'. And make sure you're clear about what YNC defines a new business to be; sometimes it can be a simple investment rather than launching a sensible multinational conglomerate. So keep this in mind when selecting the type of visa that best works for you.

PARTNERS

If you and your chap are not married, you will need to prove that you are a genuine couple. The general rule is that you'll need to prove you've lived together for at least the last 12 months. If you do need to give proof of being in a 'de facto' relationship, keep old e-mails, cards, letters, and photos – anything that shows the history of your time together.

Marrying a beloved Johnny Foreigner will always improve your chances, but the old cliché of tying the knot with a random local boy, purely for residency status should not be considered (especially if you're already going out with someone). While some less discerning young ladies are not fazed by tying the knot with some unsuspecting bloke (say Cletus the 'gator farmer, whose mother also happens to be his sister), Sensible Girls require a little more class and romance on their special day.

Likewise, if you suddenly find yourself with a doting boyfriend hours after casually mentioning you have enough points to emigrate...BE SUSPICIOUS. It is not unheard of for Sensible Girls to be duped by unscrupulous, predatory males who are after just one thing: residency! These nasty pieces of work will disappear equally as fast once the paperwork gets stamped and you will be left feeling used and abused. As always, be sensible in the run-up to your big move and steer clear of suspected love rats!

TIMING

You will also find that countries will penalise you for being 'old' (the cheek!). You may lose valuable points towards residency if you pass the ripe old age of 30. You will completely lose the chance of a two-year working visa in Oz if you exceed the big Three O. Yet another reason for getting your skates on!

Once you are granted a visa, you may be given a time limit to make use of it (i.e. it will expire if you don't go and live in YNC within the specified deadline). So it goes without saying that if you have gone to the trouble and expense of applying for the thing, you don't want to leave it too long to get out there. Doing so will only put added pressure on your timings (best case scenario), or mean that you run out of time completely and blow your chances or have to start again (disastrous case scenario).

Finally, when you have eventually waded through all of this bureaucratic nonsense diarize everything and keep copies of every scrap of correspondence and paperwork. That way, if there are any complications or problems once you've left home, you will still have everything in writing.

We're used to hearing the term illegal immigrant when referring to 'foreigners' who sneak across UK borders on the sly. But we are far less accustomed to hearing the term when referring to Brits abroad. So you might be surprised to learn that there are a lot of sneaky girls and boys out there who did NOT get their new country's paperwork signed, sealed and delivered. Rather than sneaking into their new countries illegally, more often than not, these cheeky Brits simply over-stayed their welcome (i.e. gap year students who decided that the 'gap' wasn't big enough).

Backpacking hot-spots such as Australia estimate there are literally thousands of British 'overstayers' sneaking around each year. But if you think that this might be your 'way in', think again. Even if these Overstayers don't immediately get caught in their new country, if they ever fly back to Blighty they will be busted BIG TIME on their way out. And then it will be a real case of 'game over' on the emigration front.

So, if you've tried everything (and I mean everything legal!) and you still find that you are not allowed to work in YNC, do *not* have a sneaky go anyway. It's not worth it.

Do not 'pass go'.

Do not 'collect £200'.

Return to Chapter 4.

Pick another country and try again.

You'll get there in the end!

CHAPTER 7

PLANTING SEEDS

They say a woman's work is never done...
All I'm saying is, maybe if you organised yourselves a bit better...
JIMMY CARR[1]

Your future planning consists of key points that you need to consider when finding a new life in YNC: think of this as your 'planting' checklist. The more ticks you have, the more likely it is that you'll be able to make your escape to pastures new.

Let's start with the basics.

THE PAPERWORK • Can you legally live and work in YNC?	✔
FINDING THE CASH • Can you afford it?	
FINDING A HOME • Can you find somewhere lovely to live?	
FINDING A JOB • Can you get yourself a decent job?	
FINDING A FRIEND • Do you know anyone in YNC?	
FINDING THE FUN • Have you thought about the 'fun stuff'?	

You may need to make additions and subtractions, depending on where your chosen destination lies. While the list is written in some kind of priority order, some people will find certain points far more important than others (i.e. if you're saving up to go and build yachts with your long-lost uncle in Thailand, you can tick your career and home boxes before you can tick cash).

Sometimes you may find that you can't really move on to the next point until you have the previous one in the bag. In other words, don't start eyeing up that chic downtown apartment until you can find the job to pay for it – and don't do *anything* before you know you can legally enter YNC.

It's all about future planning.

Once you've got some kind of 'running order' in place you will get an idea of how much can be achieved before you move to YNC – and how much can't. Preparation is the key, but there's no need to be a perfectionist. Once you feel you've done all you can, move on to the next category; and once you've ticked all of them and tied up your loose ends (see Chapter 8), maybe it'll be time to go!

Feel free to make unlimited sub-lists, supplementary lists, and miscellaneous additional lists.

FINDING THE CASH
Emigrating isn't cheap – but you knew that already.

SAVING
Whether it's just you and your rucksack flying to the States or the whole family relocating to Malaysia, stop shopping and start saving. A frightfully dull prospect, maybe, but try to visualise that divine Marc Jacobs cardigan as a visa application fee instead. It won't necessarily make you look fabulous, but it will take you a step closer to your dream destination.

Work on the rule that the more money you have in the bank, the more relaxed you can be with your move. You will have lots more options open to you if the fear of running out of cash is not at the forefront of your mind.

TIMING
Be honest with yourself: can you afford to do it this year? Or would it be more sensible to wait six months and have a bit more cash behind you?

Once you've started the escape plan, don't be impatient, even if you feel desperate to run away. A couple of extra months working in your current job could mean the difference between having to get work the instant you arrive in YNC, or having a couple of months grace to sort things out and really get what you want.

BANKING

On a more logistical front, try to open a bank account in YNC as soon as possible. The chances are you can do this from the UK (YNC might even have a branch here), which will be much simpler as you will have a permanent address, salary, contact numbers, etc. Speak to your own bank and they may be able to help, or at least point you in the right direction.

Once you have set this up, make sure you can access all parts of your account via the Internet. Then you will be able to transfer funds from your existing UK bank accounts with the flick of a switch and keep an eye on everything while doing so.

Finally, if you've managed to sell your UK property (and actually banked a profit in these challenging times) you will not be developing Posh or Paris's penchant for shopping. This does not give you carte blanche in the shoe department of Harvey Nics. Your savings are sacred...so step away from the plastic.

FINDING A HOME

People just *love* the idea of buying a place in the sun. Everyone wants a piece of the action. In the UK, many of us dream about living in a rustic cottage in the British countryside, with a veggie patch and some chickens. The reality is that unless you are prepared to endure a three-hour commute each morning or become a successful market gardener or egg entrepreneur, this just isn't an option for the average city gal. Do remember this simple principle in your quest to find the perfect abode abroad! Remove the soft-focus, rose-tinted sunglasses and replace with your realistic-house-hunting specs and remember that the 'house of your dreams' might be a few rental properties down the line.

RELOCATION AGENCIES

With the rising number of emigrating Brits, there are relocation agencies popping up all over the place. You will, of course, have to pay for their services, but they can prove very helpful if you don't have the time, knowledge or stamina to find somewhere to stay when you first arrive. Depending on the level of service required, they will meet you at the airport, take you to your pre-selected temporary accommodation and give you some orientation to help you feel at home. They can then assist you in searching for jobs, schools and rental properties as well as advising about more involved issues such as taxes, house buying and mortgages, which can be particularly helpful if you are a bit clueless in YNC. Finally, they can put you in touch with other expats, which can calm those post-emigration jitters when you first arrive.

'The main idea of the whole relocation package is to provide the Newbie [yep – that's you!] with information regarding the area to which they want to move to,' says expat specialist and US relocation adviser Lizzy McNaney-Juster.[2] 'It's so much easier when you can deal with someone who has already been through the process. The most useful part of any relocation is knowing someone who can point you in the right direction and not send you on a wild goose chase. Someone who has names, numbers and e-mail addresses.'

Essentially, this is information that you know (and take for granted) in the UK, but are not quite so clued-up about in YNC. As with immigration agents, shop around to find someone who has a good track record and don't be afraid to ask for accreditation.

TO RENT OR TO BUY? THAT IS THE QUESTION

Do online searches of local estate agencies and see what's out there. In these unpredictable times it's a tricky decision, but most people rent when they first arrive in Their New Country. It's less of a commitment (especially when you don't quite know what to expect), it doesn't tie you down to one location (in case you find work in another part of town) and it keeps things flexible until you find your feet and get yourself a job (which will in turn enable you to start thinking about mortgages). Get a feel for both markets and remember to factor a rental deposit into the savings you transfer over.

And speaking of renting, don't forget that it can often be more common for people to rent than purchase properties outright – especially on the Continent. So it's not a sin to forget your British obsession with land ownership and do as the Romans do.

When you look at properties for sale in London, you know that the big house in Hounslow is going to be cheaper than the tiny studio flat in Sloane Square. Don't forget that the same applies to any city. You just need to learn your areas and that's something that can only be done properly once you're out there. Even with the Credit Crunch causing havoc, there still aren't many places on this planet that are as pricey as the UK (especially London), so hopefully you will be getting better value for your money anyway. There is a lot to be said for not overly committing yourself financially to a property before you get there. You will need to work out a sensible estimate of what wage you will be able to command once you're up and running in YNC (which may have absolutely no similarity to your current UK pay packet). It's no good looking at all the swish houses and clapping your greedy little hands together with glee because your UK-based middle management job means you could almost afford two. Four syllables: i-rrel-e-vant!

And finally there's the other commitment: time. When looking at rental accommodation, work out what you think your circumstances will be in the first year. Do you want to immediately commit to a one-year lease or do you want a bit more flexibility? Would a short-term holiday rental be a good starting block? Are you expecting a huge shipment of your furniture? If so, will you need a furnished property to tide you over long term, followed shortly by an unfurnished one short term? It can get complicated, but at this stage you just need to have a running order.

FINDING A JOB
This will be one of the deciding factors as to whether or not you are going to take the plunge and move abroad, for it goes without saying that if you can't earn the dough, you ain't gonna go.

Basic questions you need to ask yourself are as follows.

• How do I intend to earn money?
• Can I get a similar job to the one I already have?
• Do I *want* to get a similar job to the one I already have?
• Can I command a similar wage to the one I already have (relatively)?
• Does my present employer have a division in My New Country? (It does happen, and it does make things much, much easier.)
• Can I start contacting prospective employers before I get there?
• Does my visa require that I absolutely MUST start contacting prospective employers before I can leave?
• If I'm planning on changing my career, am I fully equipped to do so?
• If I need to re-train, have I researched appropriate courses both at home and overseas?
• Can I afford to finance this career change, bearing in mind the already growing expense of the move?

- If I'm currently self-employed, could I continue this work if I moved abroad?

- If I am thinking of setting up my own business, have I done the sums and research so that there are not going to be any nasty shocks to scupper my plans the moment I arrive?

TIMING

As always, be flexible. If you do not have a specific job lined up for your arrival, take things step by step – especially if you are aiming for a career change. The alpaca farm/Internet café/cookery school you've always dreamt of will happen – eventually. But you might need to take the IT job in town to begin with.

If you do have a job lined up in YNC, keep the lines of communication open with your new boss. Your departure date from the UK may fluctuate a little (thanks to an overlooked spinning plate), which will affect your starting date. You don't want to annoy your new employer before you've even got there, so keeping them in the loop (rather than simply hoping for the best) is always a sensible plan.

PREPARATION

When entering YNC without a job lined up, it's always a good idea to be as ready as possible. Simple things like making sure your CV is 100 per cent up to date (see Chapter 18) means you can start applying for jobs as soon as you need to, even if you don't have decent access to a PC when you first arrive.

Are your UK qualifications recognised or relevant in YNC? It's best to check and most immigration websites will be able to guide you through what certificates, diplomas and degrees are generally accepted, as the more feathers you have in your bow, the more chance you have of securing employment.

It would also be a good plan to ask your boss to write you a glowing letter of recommendation before you leave, as agencies and employers will often require references. These people will be much happier if you can hand something over immediately, rather than them having to contact your UK office directly. Get it done on headed paper (obviously) and take a few copies with you to dish out.

Also make sure you keep a note of your boss's direct line and e-mail address, as future employers and recruitment agencies will require this if they do decide to source references independently.

Check out recruitment websites that can give you an idea of what is available and what wage to expect. Try tracking down YNC's local and national newspaper websites, as they usually have a job section online too. You may have also noticed, while researching your visa application, that immigration agencies have employment news and job links as well.

If you already know of specific companies out there that interest you, find their websites, contact their HR department and explain your situation. You may be overseas at the moment, but they might have a position coming up that's perfect for you – and you might be perfect for them. You never know your luck!

PAY

Some of you will be lucky and get a pay rise when working abroad...and some of you won't. In fact you may have to take a substantial drop in wages. It all depends on the job you do in the UK and the relative cost of living overseas. It is essential when researching your potential earnings that you take the cost of living in YNC into consideration. What looks like a dramatic pay drop on paper might actually go a lot further in your new day-to-day life, and that's what's important.

You may well be moving overseas for the sole reason of earning more cash. For example, our hard-working nurses will know that the US pays a better wage than the UK – and that's incentive enough. Alternatively, traditional tradesmen like plumbers, builders, carpenters, etc., are in great demand in countries that have certain skills shortages, so again, that particular job market will be a lucrative one to move into. And as for all the IT buffs out there, go forth and earn your fortunes!

As you can see it's well worth researching these types of trends in YNC as you might change your mind about giving up your present career – especially if you know that you'll get paid double and be able to live near the beach!

OPTIONS

Taking the job sponsorship visa option can be a great fast-track opportunity. Once you secure a position, you have the luxury of moving abroad with the knowledge that you have a guaranteed wage, a new network of colleagues, immigration paperwork signed off and possibly even a relocation package to help with costs. Getting sponsorship can depend greatly on the country to which you are applying and as we've already touched upon, will probably work on the basis that only a 'Jenny Foreigner' such as yourself will be employed if they can't fill the position from the local community.

The only real niggle with job sponsorship is that you can feel tied to the one company. You may be faced with leaving your job *and* YNC if you get sacked, made redundant or simply feel the need to resign. But don't let this put you off, as there could be the option of switching sponsors or looking at other immigration options if the worst-case scenario happens. Depending on YNC, you might just need to fill in any gaps between employment with a tourist visa. Just remind yourself that when looking for a job, choose one that you think you will enjoy (not just one that gets you residency).

If you are taking the entrepreneur route into YNC, don't forget that there are often government incentive schemes in place. When you are doing your research, check if you are eligible for a grant, or some kind of tax break. You never know.

FINDING A FRIEND

It is very easy to get bogged down in all the technicalities when moving abroad, but you'll soon realize that, while employment and paperwork are important, finding a friend will be one of the key factors in accomplishing a successful, long-term emigration... especially when it comes to us girls. It's simple, if you don't feel accepted, happy and included in your new foreign community (i.e. by making new friends), you'll end up feeling miserable, lonely and incredibly homesick. All bad...especially when you feel like you're a million miles from home. Having good friends when you live abroad, can be the difference between sacking-it-all-off and running home, or pushing through the hard times, simply because you have the support of others. So treat 'friend finding' with as much importance as the technical stuff.

THE EXISTING ONES
More often than not, people who choose to emigrate do so to be

near their friends and family. If you are lucky enough to have these connections, make sure you use them (in the nicest way possible, of course).

These people will become your negotiators, escorts, interpreters, cooks, landlords, guides, agony aunts and confidantes all rolled into one. The chance of staying with them when you first arrive will be invaluable in those first few months and their support and advice will be priceless.

Now while I only advocate the responsible 'using' of these kind and helpful foreign folk (related or not), I will say this. Don't underestimate the kindness of people. On the whole the human race is a helpful bunch (although queuing in Sainsbury's on a Friday night might make you beg to differ) and people are very proud of their countries. The fact that you have uprooted your life to live in their lovely country will make them want to prove that you were completely and utterly right to do so. Treat their kindness with respect.

If you don't have close family or friends where you are going, do you have any distant, second cousins twice removed? How about your boss's wife's hairdresser? However tenuous the link may be, take these people's contact details whenever offered.

GenXpat author, Margaret Malewski,[3] agrees that utilising friends of friends, however distant, is a good plan of attack:

'Before leaving your home country, let your acquaintances know where you are heading and ask whether they know anyone there.' Because even if the person in question is an old friend of your grandfather, 'he may have a grandchild he can introduce you to.'

In those formative weeks, if you have a problem and no one else can help you (and you can't locate the A-Team), these people can turn into real life-savers. Never underestimate the value of a friendly face when you are 'going it alone' in a strange new country.

THE NEW ONES

Whether or not you have existing friends in YNC, you will undoubtedly need a few more once you start settling in. After all, a Sensible Girl can never be too popular!

A Sensible Senior who emigrated to Zambia in the late 60's sums up the search for friends quite succinctly: 'New friends will not come and find you; you have to go out and find them.'[4] Back then, she didn't have access to the wide range of communication options we all take for granted today, so think yourselves lucky, ladies. Now that you have the Internet at your fingertips, you may as well get started early. Making friends, or should I say making *good* friends, can take a bit of time and effort, so dedicate some research time to 'friend finding', starting with expat websites, emigration forums and chat rooms relevant to YNC.

In most cases, there are hundreds of these websites knocking around and most of them will have, amongst other things, discussion forums. Forums will be divided into areas (countries/states/cities), users (single males/young mothers/teens) and topics and once you have logged your details onto their system you can post your own questions or respond to other people's. There will be plenty of: 'Hi I've just moved to Cleveland – is there anywhere I can find a decent pint of Guinness? ☺' kind of thing (my research revealed that alcohol seemed to be the uniting factor for any Brit abroad). But just start chatting and asking questions and you'll find a few friendly souls who might be best-friend material once you arrive.

And likewise, if you're looking for luurve, you can do so in cyberspace and line 'em up ready for your arrival!

FINDING THE FUN

This is another key component of any successful emigration plan and one that is often forgotten amidst the organisation and planning.

These days, one of the most common reasons for emigrating is to find a better lifestyle (work less, have more fun, get a life – that kind of thing). So you don't want to find yourself living a busy, stressful life abroad, with zero play time.

Why have you picked YNC? Are there activities that you've been looking forward to doing out there, that you can't do in the UK? Or do you secretly have a burning ambition to learn a musical instrument or foreign language and have never quite got round to doing it?

Whatever it is you are looking for, please don't lose sight of these dreams...or get so caught up in the logistics of moving abroad that you overlook them. For they will form the icing that will be piped onto your newly baked emigration cake, they will be the 'cool bits', the bits that you can brag about to everyone back home (like you weren't going to): the Detail.

If you've lived in a busy UK city all your life, you've quite possibly not had a decent hobby since you collected rubbers and played the recorder...aged seven and a half. So dig deep and think of everything you've been wanting/meaning/longing to do for all these years. What does YNC have to offer that Blighty didn't? Can you go windsurfing, mountain biking, horse riding or mountaineering? Or would you like to be more social and join the local netball, football or dragon boat racing team?

Maybe you'll be able to own the puppy/python/pot-bellied pig you always wanted.

Maybe you could volunteer to rescue dolphins or teach kids how to paint.

Whatever you wrote in your Wish List, whatever you feel you can't live without, or simply whatever you have always quite fancied, see what is out there and get excited. After all, learning to surf or abseil may never have been an option until now.

CHAPTER 8

TYING UP LOOSE ENDS

A woman is like a tea bag – you can't tell how strong she is until you put her in hot water.
ELEANOR ROOSEVELT[1]

And you thought the seed planting was tough...

In some ways, tying up all of your loose ends can be more daunting than starting your life overseas. Over there you essentially have a beautiful, blank canvas, which is waiting for you to make the first brush stroke. Back here, on the other hand, you've got a huge, messy, complicated web of a life that feels like it's going to take around 684,000 years to pick apart and get into some kind of order. Have no fear. As with any troublesome knot, the trick is to find the key tangles. After unpicking a couple of these, everything else will come apart easily. Once the whole lot has been organised, you can neatly tie up those loose ends and tidy everything away.

Once again, the plates start spinning and the lists keep rolling. Let's start with the basics.

• Tying up your finances	
• Tying up your property	
• Tying up your job	
• Tying up your car	
• Tying up your pet	
• Tying up your health	
• Tying up your stuff (and storing or shipping it)	

You will need to get your calendar up to date. Log everything: all appointments, deadlines, when you applied for things, when you paid for things, when you sent or received forms, when people contacted you, when your best friend's birthday is... EVERYTHING. Otherwise you'll end up dropping a plate.

TYING UP YOUR FINANCES

Now that your days of retail therapy are temporarily on hold and your bank account is out of the red for more than an hour, it's time to build up your finances. Picture yourself as Scrooge – albeit in make-up and a frock.

BANKS

If you have more than one UK bank account, work out which ones are a priority (e.g. accounts that will give you access once abroad or have a high interest rate for savings) and concentrate on these. You will need to keep at least one account active throughout your emigration, as it will become your financial doorway from one country to another. Whether you're receiving rent from your leased property or a £5 birthday cheque from your Aunty Dotty, if people in the UK need to pay you money they don't want to be bothered with currency changes, bank transfers and so on. Make it easy for them, and yourself.

If you have any random bank accounts that were opened by your granny when you were six, it might be time to bin the super-saver piggybank and close them. If that's all a bit radical and you would rather hang on to them, just keep a few pounds in there, print off a statement and file everything in your box file. It goes without saying that you should list all these miscellaneous accounts you leave behind, so that you don't forget where a single penny is stockpiled.

If you are moving out of the property where your bank mail was delivered, make sure you change the contact details of all remaining UK-based accounts, a reliable relative will suffice until you are more settled.

On a more basic level, nearer your departure date, check all the bank cards that you will be taking with you. If any of them are due to expire, or are so overused the signature is becoming faint (ring any bells?), order new ones. It's a lot easier to do this here rather than over there. It's also an idea to take a full cheque book with you (even though we live in the electronic age where we have Internet transfer facilities), as you can still pay people in the UK with sterling when you don't have computer access (e.g. paying your mum to do an emergency M&S knicker mail-out).

Feel free to have a chat with your new friend, the bank manager, about money matters, but a word of warning. Some banks get nervous if they think you're moving abroad for good and may even suggest that you close your accounts, which you obviously want to avoid doing for the moment. So by all means mention it, but maybe don't use the word 'permanent' just yet – after all, you never know when you might come back!

EMERGENCY MONEY – TO GET YOU OUT THERE

As you begin 'costing up' your emigration, you will start working how much your Big Move is going to cost. Whatever you are expecting to pay out over the next 12 months, be it visa applications or shipping payments, make sure you have a bit more up your sleeve. A buffer zone...a cash cushion...a sterling safety net. Whatever you want to call it, these extra funds will help you when The Unexpected pops up and bites you on the behind. Because, as you're about to learn, emigration has an annoying habit of doing that every now and then.

EMERGENCY MONEY – TO BRING YOU BACK

Looking at things from a different perspective, if emigrating makes you nervous and you have the finances, you can always stash away a little nest-egg for a different kind of emergency use. This is more for psychological reasons than anything else. It reminds you that if all else fails and if YNC turns out to be a stinking, godforsaken hell hole, then you will always have enough cash to get yourself back home and on your feet again.

Once you have decided to have this escape fund, keep it separate and *do not touch it*. Regard it a financial security blanket and deposit it in an account which will 'work for you' while you are gone. The obvious considerations of finding a good interest rate should be balanced with accessibility (especially from abroad – although this is not essential) and don't forget that you should not be paying tax on your savings while you are overseas (see next section) so don't waste time worrying about tax free options.

THE JOY OF TAX

We can't go any further without mentioning the 'T' word.

As you know, sorting out tax issues is possibly the single most tedious experience womankind has to endure. But rather than attempting to anticipate all of your tax issues (we're thinking *War and Peace* again), I have picked out a few key Tax Topics for your consideration (and you can always log on to the government's website to delve a little deeper).

I'll start with a crowd pleaser.

To keep your spirits up, you might be surprised to learn that there is a strong chance Mr Taxman (or Mrs Taxwoman, for that matter) could owe *you* some money for a change! Each year, our chums at Her Majesty's Customs and Revenue (HMRC), rack up squillions of pounds of unclaimed tax refunds. So it's up to you to work out if you're owed anything. To find out, you will need to fill in a P85 form,[2] which you can download from the HMRC website (**www.hmrc.gov.uk**), and the Inland Revenue will let you know the rest. (Note that you can only be refunded once you have left your UK employment, however.)

If you are selling a property, flash car or ridiculously large designer wardrobe, you may have a lump sum of money heading your way, and as a rule, Mr Taxman would usually try to take a big fat helping of your savings' interest. But with non-resident status on the horizon, fill out a R105[3] form (c/o HMRC) and hand this in to your local bank or building society. They should see to it that once you are out of the country, all your interest will be tax free. Not really an issue for those puny super-saver accounts, but a big deal if you've just sold your two-bedroom flat!

Another tax consideration is whether you will continue to receive some kind of income while you are living out of the country. If so, your first mission will be to find out whether YNC partakes in a Double Taxation (DT) Agreement.[4] The UK has negotiated DT treaties with over 100 countries, so the chances are you might be able to claim exemption from being taxed in Blighty, but do your homework thoroughly.

Maybe you are renting out that two-bedroom flat in Knightsbridge rather than selling it! If so, you'll need to check out the Non-resident Landlord Scheme,[5] as this could help you receive your rental income without tax being deducted. But this will depend on many variables, such as how much your rent is, whether you have a letting agent, and so on.

You see – tax is tricky.

There are plenty of other tax issues such as capital gains tax, tax on UK investment income, tax on UK pensions if you're a

Sensible Senior...but all the information is available (and updated) on the HMRC website, so educate yourself on such matters and let them know that you're leaving the country.

OTHER TRICKY MONEY STUFF

If you thought tax was boring, wait until you start on your National Insurance (NI) contributions!

Now that you're leaving the country indefinitely (although, granted, you're not exactly sure how long for), your NI contributions will probably grind to a halt.

What you need to do is get yourself a Retirement Pension Forecast by filling in form CA3638,[6] which will add up your contributions to date and calculate what kind of a pension you can expect to receive when you retire. You will also be able to receive advice on how you can improve this figure and get the most out of your pension. The next consideration is working out whether you wish to make voluntary contributions from overseas (regular 'top-up' payments); in doing so you still be entitled to your pension, even though you no longer live in the UK. To complicate things further, countries in the EEA (and many others) have reciprocal agreements so you can go through their system and retain your entitlements. And for the more mature girls in our midst, be aware that transferring pensions to countries such as Australia, New Zealand and Canada will mean if you are about to draw it (or if you're already drawing it), once you emigrate that rate will be frozen. This means you will not benefit from the cost-of-living increases that UK residents would benefit from.[7] Big bummer!

I could go on, but as I keep saying, this little book was never meant to get too hung up on 'the paperwork', as there are plenty of helpful websites out there which will guide you through the complicated stuff. There is, of course, an alternative to boring yourself senseless with all of this tax business, and that is calling in the services of a friendly financial adviser. And this is probably the most sensible piece of advice I can offer, as speaking to an expert is important when dealing with your financial future.

It goes without saying that you need to find a good one.[8] They will be able to look at your individual circumstances and advise you on exactly what you should and shouldn't be doing with your finances. Don't worry about running out of conversation; there will be plenty of things to talk about. Personal pension plans, outstanding loans or credit card debts, shares or premium bonds, savings accounts, interest, the joys of tax...basically everything we've touched upon. Don't put these things off until the last minute either, as you could end up losing money in the long run – and THAT wouldn't be sensible at all.

THE EXCHANGE RATE

Finally, it is essential that you become very well acquainted with the exchange rate in YNC – especially in these challenging financial times. Get into the habit of checking it on a regular basis via the Internet. You might be surprised at how things can fluctuate and raising your awareness will stand you in good stead when you finally make the decision to transfer your sterling into your new currency.

If you have a big savings account, getting a good rate of exchange can dictate whether you lose or gain a substantial amount of money (we could be talking thousands). There are plenty of foreign exchange brokers out there who will assist you with these financial transfers. They can help you secure a fixed rate that won't suddenly change by the time your local bank pulls its finger out or your house sale goes through, thus enabling you to securely move your savings overseas at an exchange rate that you're happy with. If there is a considerable delay in accessing money that you wish to exchange (e.g. a delay in a house sale), a deposit may be needed, but this could be a small inconvenience compared to what would happen if you were moving your money over to YNC with a lousy exchange rate.

Alternatively, you can arrange for monthly transfers to be transferred over to YNC (if you're paying rent or receiving pension payments, for example) which can be 'locked in' with an agreed exchange rate...giving peace of mind and saving on bank fees. Leading foreign exchange service providers such as HiFX (**www.hifx.co.uk**) are experts in all of these matters. But whoever you choose, run through the following checklist when selecting a company to transfer your cash.

- Check they are regulated.
- Check their charges.
- Check the rate you are quoted is the rate you will actually receive.
- Check they hold your money in segregated client trust accounts.

Remember, you can work the exchange rate to your advantage if you are lucky (but it can also work against you if you're not). Be careful, pay close attention, be clear about the maximum (and minimum) rate that you're hanging out for and have your money lined up and ready to go as rates can vary from hour to hour and you will need to catch it when it's favourable.

When discussing finances with Brits who have emigrated, a lot of people prefer *not* to move their money out of the UK until they're a bit more settled and sorted. It can often make sense to leave most of your capital in a British account until you are in real need of it (e.g. when you are ready to buy a property, car or Gucci handbag). And although sterling is currently taking a bit of a beating thanks to the GFC, historically it usually comes good in the end and is one of the stronger currencies. So until you are 100 per cent sure that you want to give it a go in YNC, your money should stay over here in your bank, tucked up safe and sound.

TYING UP YOUR PROPERTY

Before we get to grips with home ownership and the decisions that will need to be made, we should start with the easy stuff first. The Sensible Girls who didn't quite manage (or choose) to get their feet onto the property ladder and so live either at home, with family or friends, or simply rent. And with property prices doing what they're doing, there are plenty of 'ladies-what-lease' out there!

RENTING
The good news is that you girls don't really have too much decision-making to do. It's more a case of packing your bags and bidding adios to your housemates. The main thing to consider is your timing, which boils down to aligning your 'moving out dates' with your 'leaving the country dates'. To avoid squabbles over wine stains on the Axminster, leave a substantial gap between

moving out and leaving the country, as this will give you time to get your deposit back if there are any issues with your landlord. It will also ease the pressure from trying to get all of your emigration plans in sync (your life is full of spinning plates!) and give you a bit of breathing space. Obviously you will need to find an accommodating friend or family member to offer their spare room for the last week or so of your time in the UK, but at least you will be able to do so knowing that your Property Loose End has been tied neatly away.

If appropriate, get references from your landlord saying what a perfect tenant you were. They're not absolutely essential, but they may come in handy when trying to find your first rental property in YNC, as you won't have the usual people around you who can provide character references.

Sensible Girls still living at home can skip the rest of this section and feel smug (which is not often the case when comparing yourselves with the lucky souls who have managed to bag themselves a UK property), so skip away and enjoy.

Now it gets a bit more involved.

OWNING YOUR OWN PROPERTY

Hmmm...you can pack your designer wardrobe – hell, you can pack your entire wardrobe – but what are you going to do with your house?

The two main options you will be considering are either to sell or to let and – as you know if you've already started trying to work out what to do – there are numerous considerations to mull over.

SELLING	LETTING
Pros • You may stand to make a profit of some kind and this could give you a large lump sum of well-needed cash for your emigration. • Depending on your lump sum, you will be able to put down a deposit on a property abroad. This will give some kind of security in YNC plus a future investment. • While the UK housing market is up and down, it is relatively strong in comparison to most other countries in the Top Ten Emigration Destinations, so you are still likely to get more for your money abroad. • You will make a clean break and not have any bills or worry associated with letting a property while living abroad. • As a result of your house sale, you may have a large sum of cash residing in a high interest account (they do still exist), which will give you some kind of monthly income (depending on the size of your savings and interest rate).	*Pros* • You will have a property to come back to (should you wish to), or a property to sell at a later date, when your situation is clearer (and house prices are more stable). • Your feet are still firmly on the UK property ladder and your money is 'working for you', rather than sitting in a bank account. • Your tenant could be paying off your mortgage and bills and you may even end up with a monthly income if you're lucky. • You may choose to rent your property furnished and therefore will not incur big storage costs.

SELLING	LETTING
Cons	*Cons*
• A weaker housing market will influence your profit margin when selling the house and affect how much cash you can take with you. Timing is paramount.	• You will not have the funds available to emigrate that selling provides.
• You will not have a place of your own to come back to, should you so choose.	• You have no guarantee that you will find tenants immediately. And once you do, you have no guarantee that they will be reliable or respectful.
• You have taken your feet off the UK property ladder and will no longer have an investment in Blighty.	• Because you're abroad, it is advisable to rent through an agency. However, they will take a substantial monthly percentage of your rent (10–15 per cent, depending on their services).
• You will have to remove all of your worldly possessions from your property and arrange for them to go into storage.	• You will also need to invest some cash into meeting all the agency's rental requirements (redecorating, meeting safety standards, special house insurance, etc.). And there will be repairs and maintenance to pay as well.
• If, after time, you decide to re-buy a property in the UK, you will incur all the usual expenses associated with house buying...but without the benefits of having recently sold a UK property.	• You will probably need to let your mortgage lender know you wish to let your home and, annoyingly, some might not be happy about you doing so and leaving the country indefinitely. So check first.
• Fluctuating financial markets are greatly affecting our banks – which makes selecting where to stash our cash more stressful.	

You see! There are a million and one things to consider, so rather than try to cover everything in this book, I'll leave that to the experts. Talk to estate agents, rental agencies, and financial planners. If you are unsure about the ins and outs of renting out your property start off by having a read through the Citizen's Advice Bureau advice guide (**www.adviceguide.org.uk**) as they can help with the basics. Don't be afraid of getting more than one opinion. Keep an eye on prices in your area and compare them with the property market in the area you intend to move to keep yourself as well informed as possible.

Once you have reached a decision, don't blab to all and sundry that you are moving abroad, for this nugget of information might weaken your negotiating position. To explain: if Mr & Mrs Bloggs want to buy your house and know you are vacating the country ASAP, they are going to try to knock you down on the asking price or even suggest that you might like to throw in the white goods for free. People are opportunistic and can be very cheeky when it comes to doing business, so play your cards close to your chest and hold your nerve.

Most importantly, whatever you decide to do, there isn't necessarily a 'right' or 'wrong' answer to the situation in which you find yourself, it just depends what your priorities are. It is also important to note that, contrary to popular belief, you will *not* drop dead if you remove your feet from the UK property ladder...life does manage to carry on!

And, anyway, as you can see from the chart, great opportunities can arise from either solution. You'll make things work for you, and that's all that matters.

TYING UP YOUR JOB

Since you have already made the decision to leave your job, the only real loose end to deal with here is deciding when to spill the beans.

Those in favour of letting the cat out of the proverbial handbag early on will need to consider a few of the following things before blabbing.

As we already know, visa/work permit applications can take a long time, but once your office knows your plans, they are unlikely to give you any further promotions, pay rises or send you on courses, etc. If you feel that one of these 'treats' is just around the corner, keep quiet for a while longer if you can, even if that means keeping a few secrets.

On the other hand, you may find that you need a written statement from your current employer to process a visa application: in which case unless you get him or her stupendously drunk or brush up on your forgery skills (I jest), you will need to reveal your hand.

Investigate the chances of being given voluntary redundancy before you open your mouth. It goes without saying that the possibility of actually getting paid to leave your job would be a marvellous thing indeed.

In the run-up to your departure, do not use up any more annual leave unless it is absolutely necessary. Remember those precious days are worth a lot more to you in cash now* and you can always take a break en route to YNC if you get the chance.

If you have developed a loathing for your current employer and feel that this could be your one chance to get a few things off your chest – DON'T. While moving to another country seems to offer a come-back-free opportunity to seek vengeance, avoid the temptation. Aside from the possibility that you may need their recommendation for your visa application; you will probably need their references for future job and rental applications. So if the urge to draw attention to your supervisor's evil-smelling halitosis at the next internal meeting is strong, bite your tongue and don't burn bridges.

Finally, all employees know that at least 40 per cent of time at one's desk should be spent sending personal e-mails, fiddling around on Facebook and making pointless purchases on eBay. Unfortunately, employers do not have the same mentality. I've already mentioned the fact that emigrating will demand a lot of Google hours, so just remember that once your secret is out, your research will need to be a little more covert.

---

* Obviously, do this only if your friendly HR department is willing to swap leftover holidays for cash.

TYING UP YOUR CAR

Whether your car gets to emigrate with you greatly depends on where you are emigrating to. For example, if you are moving to the Continent it can easily tag along, but if you are flying to the States, things aren't so straightforward.

THE PAPERWORK

Sensible Girls are allowed to drive in European Community/EEA countries using a valid UK driver's licence, although depending on YNC, you may be required to exchange it for an EEA national licence once you become a resident.[9]

Certain countries require the use of an International Driving Permit (IDP), which must be obtained *before* you leave Blighty. Motoring organisations like the RAC or AA provide details of which countries require IDPs and then process your application. This will be valid for one year from the date of issue, but it can be post-dated by up to three months, so that it can be valid from your date of departure – which is handy. Remember that you will still need to present your UK driver's licence alongside the IDP, so keep both of them together.[10]

Once you arrive in YNC, look into getting hold a 'foreign driver's licence' as soon as possible. Partly because your IDP will expire after a year, but more importantly because some countries will penalise you for not quickly switching over to using one of their licences...for which the penalty can be re-sitting your driving test. The horror! So if doing five-point turns, with a non-English-speaking instructor, on the wrong side of the road doesn't appeal, keep a close eye on your driving paperwork.

Finally, if you will be insuring a vehicle once you have settled in YNC, make sure you get a letter from your current car insurers stating how many years of 'no claims' you have racked up. If you've been a good girl behind the wheel, you could be rewarded for your sensible driving with your new policy

SHIPPING

If YNC is further afield than Europe and you are unable to simply drive your car to its new home, you might want to consider employing the services of a car specialist who can assist you in shipping your vehicle overseas. But make sure it is worth the expense. If YNC is somewhere like the US, you could be better off sticking it on Auto Trader, rather than wasting a fair amount of your savings transporting it to a country where 've-hee-cals' are ten-a-penny.

On the flip-side, there are certain circumstances where cars can be worth more in foreign countries. For example, Australians are rather partial to a Beamer and everyone is rather partial to an Aston Martin. If it's all getting a bit confusing, simply work on the premise that the flashier the car, the better its chances of having a successful emigration, and you should be on the right track. Likewise, toying with the idea of shipping your mum's second-hand Vauxhall Corsa should be thought of as being on the wrong track. If you're unsure, you can always log onto the car classified pages of YNC's online newspapers to get a feel for how much your car will be worth overseas.

Check up on shipping costs and don't forget import taxes. Think about spare parts and garage costs once it's on the streets of YNC. Also try to cast your mind forward to the re-sale of your car once abroad as the locals of YNC (and this goes especially for the US) might not be interested in a car that has a 'stick shift', no aircon and a steering wheel that's on the 'wrong' side.

If you *do* decide to export your car, you will need to notify the DVLA and fill out a few more forms. Make sure that it complies with all of YNC's vehicle regulations and that it is fully insured[11]

– but a vehicle shipping specialist will be able to advise you on such matters.

As with every aspect of your decision-making, be sensible when working out whether your nippy-little-run-around needs to emigrate with you and remember that it can be of far more use to you in the form of hard cash, than costing you a bomb trying to give it on an extended holiday.

Looking at things from a more pedestrian perspective you may not own a car...or even have got round to learning to drive yet. If you live in London or any other large city, that's totally understandable. What's the point? You can read your newspaper on the train, there's nowhere to park and, quite honestly, a space hopper would get you into the centre of town quicker during rush hour.

But be warned that if you don't drive in countries like the US (New York City being an exception of course!) or Australia, you may find yourself being forcibly manhandled into a strait-jacket as these countries rely heavily on their vehicles and consider anyone walking distances above 200 metres stark raving mad.

Would it be worth putting yourself through an intensive driving course before you leave? Or would it be more sensible to learn in YNC (especially if they drive on the 'wrong' side of the road)?

TYING UP YOUR PET

Just because YOU are moving overseas, doesn't mean that Rover or Whiskers should be deposited into the nearest pound! Far from it, as these days it is relatively easy to emigrate with your beloved pet if you want to...but the question is, do THEY want to?

As with the previous section, making the decision as to whether to emigrate with your pet depends greatly on where you are emigrating to and what type of pet you have. For example, if Whiskers is in her mid-twenties and looking at the prospect of emigrating to New Zealand, you might want to re-consider retiring the old gal with a UK-based friend or relative, as it's simply not fair to uproot pets in their twilight years and expect them to readjust to a totally alien world. Likewise, if YNC has a hot or humid climate, this can cause unnecessary distress to pets who are a little set in their ways and used to the cooler climes of the UK.

Any pet who is of a very nervous disposition can also have a particularly miserable experience, especially flying long distances, as they will be boxed up, placed in the hold of the aircraft and left alone (with a fair amount of noise) for quite a few hours. But that said, plenty of dogs and cats emigrate with their 'mums and dads' every year, and arrive at the other end, bright eyed and bushy tailed. So if you feel that they are up to the task, you need to start working through their paperwork.

GETTING STARTED

The best place for you and your fluffy to get started is with the Department for Environment Food and Rural Affairs (DEFRA), who have some clear guidelines as to what you will need to do.

First of all, you need to remember that while it is easy for you and your fellow humans to return to The Motherland at the drop of a hat, your fluffy will be forced to undergo a stricter re-entry policy – namely UK quarantine – which is where the Pet Travel Scheme (PETS; see **www.defra.gov.uk/animalh/quarantine/ pets/index.htm**) comes into play. This scheme allows your fluffy to avoid long quarantine periods when returning from abroad. Countries participating in PETS are most parts of Europe and many non-EU countries.[12]

To be eligible, Fluffy will need to:

- be fitted with a microchip (your vet can do this);
- be vaccinated against rabies;
- be blood tested by an EU-approved laboratory;[13]
- not have visited any non-approved country for at least six months, prior to re-entering the UK;
- be issued with a Pet Passport by your vet (sweet!);
- travel via PETS-approved sea, air and rail routes (all listed on the PETS website);
- be treated for tapeworm and ticks no less than 24 hours (but no more than 48) before checking in with a PETS-approved carrier for the journey BACK to Blighty.

The PETS website has all the information you need, including a directory of recommended carriers and a full list of all the countries that participate in the scheme, which includes countries in the EU and further afield. Be aware that spaces are limited on PETS-approved carriers, so you should book early to guarantee a time slot that works for you.

Once you have worked out whether Fluffy can join the PETS club, you will have to fill out a few forms. Don't be surprised if your pet ends up with more paperwork than you do and consider utilising the services of a pet relocation specialist, who will be able to advise you on the intricacies of your pet's travel arrangements.

When all of the formalities are over, you can start concentrating on making sure Fluffy has the most stress-free emigration possible, so here are a few tips.

• Make sure your pet is as fit and healthy as possible to withstand the journey.
• Allow your pet to familiarise itself with their travel box prior to actually travelling. If they can get used to it before the stressful journey begins, they will feel more settled once they are on their way.
• Have some kind of blanket or cushion to put in their travel box. Choose something that has a familiar smell and that your pet associates with the comfort and security of home.
• Give them a light meal a few hours before travelling, not immediately before they depart.

- Give your pet the chance to spend a penny (or have a nice long walk) before they have to go into their travel box.

- You will not be allowed to give them any kind of tranquiliser to knock them out when flying.

- If your cat gets bored easily, buy a pet mouse as a travelling companion.[†]

- If you are travelling on a ferry route, arrive at the port early so that your vehicle can be positioned in the best place in the hold for the welfare of your pet.

- If your pet is travelling with you, make the trip overnight as your pet will be used to snoozing through the wee small hours and should sleep through a lot of the journey.

- If your pet is travelling in your vehicle, remember to take regular breaks for them to stretch their legs and have a toilet break.

- If YNC is hot, don't leave your discombobulated pet in your airless vehicle for longer than is absolutely necessary.

Depending on your pet's individual emigrating circumstances, they may have to stay in quarantine for a substantial period of

---

† OK, don't do that, I just wanted to make sure you were paying attention!

time once they arrive in YNC. This will be pretty much like the cattery or kennel you would put Fluffy in if you were going on holiday. It's a nice idea to try to pay them a visit during their stay (check first, but this is usually allowed) as they will have gone through a fair bit of stress and will be wondering where the hell they (and you) are. As well as all of the aforementioned expenses, paying for Fluffy's food and board (plus vet check-ups) while in quarantine should also be taken into consideration.

Although emigrating with your pet is not rocket science and (depending on the locality of YNC) isn't as torturous as it may have been a few years ago, you really must sit down and work out what is best for your four-legged friend, rather than selfishly deciding that Fluffy must emigrate because you want them to. Put their feelings first.

TYING UP YOUR HEALTH

Aside from a pathological aversion to filling in forms and a bad case of insomnia, you probably feel pretty good. But that's irrelevant, I'm afraid, as you still need to pay a visit to your doctor.

Even though you will have a practising GP somewhere in the vicinity of your newly chosen future home, you'd probably prefer to avoid paying them a visit upon arrival as there will be a million and one other things you will be taking care of. But, things that we take for granted in the UK, such as free contraceptive pills, might not be so readily available, or even free in YNC. So it doesn't hurt to stock up on a few items before you go. If there are any niggling health issues that you've not quite got round to talking to your GP about, now is the time. Do you need a top-up prescription, any vaccinations, a smear test or mammogram? Get these things out of the way so you don't have to worry about them for the first few months when you're trying to get settled in YNC.

The same goes for the dentist, optometrist, podiatrist, nutritionist and any other 'ist' who services you on a regular basis.

You may need to undergo a full medical for your residency application, but do not treat this as an opportunity to have 'one last check-up'. You will have to go to a pre-specified doctor (not necessarily your own) and they will certainly not be interested in your athlete's foot or waxy lug-holes. They just want to make sure you're not going to keel over with chronic heart disease upon entering their country and become a burden on their own healthcare system. So treat the medical and your own medical issues as separate entities, and get them both sorted as soon as you can.

Make sure you have a good understanding of what healthcare you can expect to get in YNC too. Some countries will require you to pay for private healthcare, some have a reciprocal agreement with the UK and offer basic services for free and others have a very limited medical service indeed. Could a good medical health insurance be a sensible (or even essential) back-up plan to start with? Do you need to look into paying for a private medical and dental policy upon arriving in YNC?

Finally, I'm always a firm believer in trying to leave the 'exit door' ajar rather than slamming it shut behind you. So be careful how you approach your GP if you feel you want to discuss moving abroad. While you have every right to rock up and get a copy of personal medical records from your GP and dentist, they then have every right to remove you from their register as a result of your leaving the area. Now, depending on your relationship with your doctor (maybe they're a lifelong family friend, maybe they're not), just think ahead. If you feel you'd like to stay on their register until you have a better idea of where your life is going to end up...maybe leave things as they are for the next few months and don't mention the 'permanent' word just yet.

TYING UP YOUR STUFF

It's time to roll up your sleeves and get down and dirty.

Whether you still live at home, rent or own your own place, you are about to embrace the principle of 'less is more'. Before you can emigrate elegantly you will need to de-clutter your life and thin out that bulging wardrobe and everything from those grimy old curtains, that drawer full of odds and sods in the kitchen, those designer jeans you can no longer squeeze into, to discarded IKEA shelving. You will be making some harsh choices in order to reach the Zen-like state of Possession Nirvana.

The first step towards this Nirvana is that of purging your property. In other words, getting rid of stuff you no longer need, want or have any use for. You must be systematic and strong in selecting what must stay and what needs to go.

THE STUFF THAT 'NEEDS TO GO'

You have a few choices, some which offer the 'quick 'n' easy' solution and others that may reimburse you with a bit of cash.

THE BIN

- **Anything that is too awful to give away, sell, hide, bury or donate.**
- **Anything that is broken, torn, split, damaged, unidentifiable or smells odd.**
- **Anything that belongs to your partner and is devoid of taste.‡**
- **Anything that is stuffed into your drawer full of rubbish.**
- **Anything that IS rubbish.**

THE CHARITY SHOP

Anything that is clean and in good working order, that you don't wish to try to sell, but do not want to simply bin.

---

‡   To avoid detection, blame storage company at later date.

THE CAR BOOT SALE

The vast majority of people who regularly frequent car boot sales are, on the whole, stingy and a teensy bit sad.[§] These people may never fully appreciate the meaning of the word 'designer'. A bag is a bag in their eyes and whether it's Balenciaga or BHS, they're offering you 50p and that's final! For this reason alone, you should avoid including any highly desirable clothing, shoes or accessories (give it to charity or sell it as vintage instead).

Note that you are only allowed to include this category if you have already researched local car boot sales and fully intend to pay a visit to one. Otherwise this exercise will result in a new pile of carrier bags being shoved into the back of your wardrobe. Remember that you are *de-cluttering* your life, not just shuffling things around. And do not buy any more clutter at the sale, for obvious reasons.

THE VINTAGE CLOTHING STORE

We will overlook the fact that if an item really is vintage, you should probably be wearing it.

As with car boot sales, you must have researched vintage buyers before embarking on this wardrobe exorcism as they can be very selective and know what they're looking for. Vintage clothing and jewellery collector Alison Henley explains:[14]

'People need to anticipate what will evolve into a fabulous vintage piece – and what won't. Sadly, I get a lot of people who mistake tat for vintage and get quite offended when I try to explain to them that there is a difference. You need have a good look at what you're offering and ask yourself the following questions.

---

§ Apologies for the gross generalisation...but come on, you know it's true!

> - Is it fabulous and would I want to wear it (if I wasn't trying to sell it)?
> - Is it in good condition?
> - Does it have a designer label? (This is preferred, but not essential.)
> - Does it have original packaging? (This adds value and authenticity to the piece.)
> - Is it a sensible size? Extremely large or small sizes are harder to sell and therefore less appealing.'

If you have answered 'yes' to most of the above and have located a potential buyer, start the bidding and make sure you get a price that you are satisfied with. Try to avoid selling items on consignment as you don't get the cash upfront and may have left the country before your stuff ever gets sold. Feel free to haggle and if you think you're being ripped off or you're simply not happy with the money they offer you, don't be shy. Take everything home and redistribute to different piles...or friends. At least you tried!

THE ADVERTISEABLE STUFF

Whether you've decided to sell your washing machine in *Loot*, your exercise bike in the local rag or your hamster cage on eBay, only sell stuff you are sure that you want to get rid of. Be wary about selling things you might find yourself replacing once you are settled in YNC. It could be false economy. The chances are you won't get a fraction of what you originally paid (or what you will have to pay again, once you replace them after the move). So ask yourself if they are worth the storage space...and go from there.

Another increasingly popular (and ethical) option is that of recycling your belongings (rather than flogging them). Websites such as Freecycle (**www.uk.freecycle.org**) allow members to give away things they no longer want, as well as get hold of stuff they do want. The obvious danger with this clever concept is that undisciplined Sensible Girls end up just swapping stuff around, rather than getting rid of it. So if you do use this 21st-century version of The Multi-Coloured Swap Shop, choose wisely as you only have a limited amount of space when emigrating.

WARDROBE MAINTENANCE

Sadly, it's a well-known fact that most girls, sensible or not, turn into raging hoarders when it comes to organising their wardrobes. Rather than ridding themselves of potential crimes of fashion, hoarders spend hours nostalgically pondering over offending items of clothing, before shoving the unworn garment straight to the back of their wardrobe, only to be forgotten for another couple of years. Useless!

'If you want to look fabulous, your wardrobe has to look fabulous too,' says Oonagh Brennan,[15] fashion director of *Company* magazine, 'and wardrobe organisation is the key, especially if you are about to ship everything overseas.

'Set aside an afternoon, switch off your mobile, put on some good music and remove *everything* from your wardrobe. Not just clothing – but shoes, bags, accessories, underwear, etc. You will then need to try on and evaluate each item and decide whether you will still wear it or, more importantly, look good wearing it!

'Make sure you throw away anything you haven't worn for 12 months.'¶ This should include clothing that still has the price tags on, clothing that you can no longer fit into and clothing

---

¶ Trying things on and dancing around in front of your mirror before taking them off again doesn't count.

that you've been thinking 'might come back in fashion'...but probably won't.

'Don't double up on things unless they are basics (e.g. white vests). Choose your favourite one and lose the others.

'Anything dirty or damaged must be dry-cleaned or repaired. It will be no good to you otherwise.' Keep hold of the dry-cleaning packaging as it will come in very handy when storing or packing your clothing. Get your shoes re-heeled and any clothing alterations done. Otherwise you will be emigrating with things that you can't immediately wear, increasing the likelihood of them being pushed to the back of your (foreign) wardrobe.

Once you've removed the clothing clutter, you should be left with a wonderful, *wearable* wardrobe. But, as Oonagh points out, your renovation is not over yet. How you replace and re-store everything will determine whether your wardrobe maintains its makeover:

'Always use wooden hangers; they are sturdier, much kinder to your clothes and they look good too. You don't have to be too anal about putting clothes into colours and themes, but it helps to have sections (e.g. coats/jackets, jeans/trousers) together so you don't forget about things. Likewise, try to limit yourself to one item per hanger. Overloading means you can't find things easily and you have to iron things that get squashed and crumpled. Keep precious shoes in their boxes to avoid them getting dusty or damaged. Rather than folding things when packing, make sure you request a Wardrobe Storage Box, which will allow clothing to hang in storage. Look after your clothes properly – and you'll always look great!'

THE STUFF YOU WANT TO KEEP

OK, so now that you've haggled, donated and eliminated your way to Possession Nirvana, you should have a house full of things that you want to keep. You now have to decide *how* and *where* you want to keep everything. You have three main options:

1. STORING BELONGINGS IN PARENTS'/RELATIVES'/FRIENDS' HOUSES

Do your parents/relatives have a big loft, garage or spare room? Can they look after your belongings until further notice – even if that includes a truckload of furniture and a skip full of shoes?

If the answer is 'yes', keep a catalogue of everything and if you've got a lot of stuff, try not to split everything up too much when storing with loved ones. It may be easy to remember who has what now, but you are probably going to forget where everything is after a couple of months.

This is the easiest and cheapest option, but it isn't a permanent solution, as you'll have to work out what to do with all of your gubbins at a later date – especially if your parents lose the use of their garage while you're making up your mind.

2. LEAVING BELONGINGS IN YOUR PROPERTY AND LETTING IT OUT

If you have decided to rent your property out as furnished, you will still only want to leave the basics.

Original artwork, fancy ornaments or antique furniture are not exactly the best things to be leaving behind. So just make sure anything that stays is robust, replaceable...or cheap.

If you are letting your property through an agency, be aware that your furniture must meet certain fire regulatory standards. If you have a sofa that is likely to spontaneously combust at the mere sniff of a tea light, you need to change it. Talk to your rental agency before you make any hasty purchases.

3. PAYING FOR STORAGE (WITH A VIEW TO SHIPPING YOUR BELONGINGS)

Paying for the services of a storage/shipping company is the most popular emigrating option when stashing and transporting your stuff.

After all, they come and pack everything up, take it away and store it indefinitely. Then they can either ship everything out to you or hold on to it for your return (depending on how things go abroad). This means you can try living in YNC for as long as you want without committing yourself to the expense of having all your belongings shipped out.

When you feel settled and confident enough, you can just pick up the phone and arrange for everything to be put on the first boat heading in your direction. Alternatively, everything can stay where it is and you can return and pick up where you left off. You will, of course, be paying a monthly fee for this privilege, but don't be put off by this as there are some reasonable deals out there which might not cost as much as you'd expect.

Most companies will come round to your house and give you a free quotation, so it's certainly worth having a chat with someone and don't be afraid to shop around and get a few quotes. Make sure they are a reputable removal company by checking credentials, such as whether they have a quality standards mark or are members of the British Association of Removers.

Once you select your removals company, they will help you decide whether you need a Full or Groupage container. A Full container will be only filled with your stuff. A Groupage container (as the name suggests) requires you to share the storage with another client. Having your own container is more expensive, and some would argue, more secure, as the container only travels from A to B and is therefore far more likely to arrive with everything still in it. If you can only fill part of a container (Groupage), make sure you check about how the other belongings in your container will affect your security and time of dispatch.

Remember to ask about insurance, as this can often bump up the original quote. You will need to take out different types of insurance, depending on whether you choose to ship your stuff over or not. Unbelievable as it may sound, containers do fall off container ships in bad weather from time to time, so those few extra pounds are definitely worth it. Don't forget to check how long the actual shipping will take either, as this may influence further decision-making.

If you are confident about your move and have a property lined up, you can send your belongings on ahead so they will be waiting for you upon arrival – for a price. The choice is yours: just make sure you get a good deal and remember there is always room for negotiation.

Once all of the negotiations are out of the way, you can get down to the nitty-gritty and start working out what you want to store/ ship. You've already had a basic run-down on how to get rid of all the stuff you don't need/want/have space for, so now you need to work your way around the house deciding what will emigrate with you (and what will stay).

For example, it may seem sensible to ship all of your electrical goods, but what if the voltage is not the same in YNC? You could be shipping over your white goods for no reason and wasting valuable space in your container. Likewise, if something is on its last legs and threatens to break down at the slightest whiff of foreign shores, don't waste the storage space on it!

Have you considered that you might not see your possessions again for quite a few months – even a year or so? Can you do with out them for that long? It is easy to shove all the boring things like bedding and towels into storage, but you are going to need some of these items pretty soon after you arrive in YNC. You won't be able to live in that five-star chi-chi hotel you've initially booked yourself in to forever! And, if you replace these things once you are out there, you're just wasting money by doubling up.

Once you have walked around your home and decided what you would like to take with you, it's time to call in the professionals.

PACKING POINTERS

- Prior to the storage company's arrival, decide whether you wish to pack your belongings or let the removal men do it. Remember that they are the experts and packing up delicate crockery and precious heirlooms is their job – so why add to your workload? That said, packing your belongings yourself may affect your insurance cover, so speak to your storage company and be clear about your situation.

- When booking the removal date, try to avoid bank holidays and school holidays, as they are most likely to be fully booked.

- For peace of mind, if you have a small child or pet, park them with a friend or relative for the day as they will only get in the way.

- Make sure the removal van has decent access to your house. This might mean sweet-talking a few neighbours to bagsie a good parking spot.

- Dismantle self-assembly furniture and take down all curtains, fixtures and fittings that you want stored *before* the removal men arrive.

- Keep passports and tickets, important documentation, medication, stuff you will need between now and your departure date, e.g. children's toys (should you have children), this book and anything else that you *don't* want packing out of the way. Have a 'no go' zone where you stash all of these contraband items and clearly explain to all of the removal men that they must not go anywhere near them.

- Check with your removal company that you don't have anything which might cause problems with the customs department of YNC. Otherwise you may end up footing the bill for your sheepskin rug or Balinese fertility mask to be zapped with gamma rays. When everything is ready to pack, make sure there are no traces of soil, organic matter or vegetation. These kind things can really freak out customs in some countries that are rather sensitive to outbreaks of foot and mouth or bird flu. So make sure those designer wellies are scrubbed until they are squeaky clean.

- If you have an attic or loft, don't expect the removal men to clamber up there and start working through your old record collection. Have everything sorted, boxed and easily accessible before they get there, as they will probably not be permitted to venture up there otherwise.

- Electrical goods such as cookers, washing machines, etc., need to be disconnected, cleaned and drained before they are due to be moved.

- A nice cup of tea is always appreciated...and you get brownie points for biscuits!

Tidying all of your belongings away can be exhausting, annoying and incredibly stressful, but don't give up and throw the whole lot in a skip (tempting as it may seem). You must be ruthless, but you don't want to be too cavalier and throw the baby out with the bath water. After all, we are talking about all your worldly possessions. If you have kids, be very careful about what you leave behind, as children will be craving familiarity when they first arrive in YNC. Good packing will deal with the emotional as well as the practical. Just be sensible!

Think of it as a giant jigsaw puzzle, working out which piece goes where. Essentially you are trying to think ahead and take into consideration every eventual outcome of your move. If you pack up your belongings and keep your options open, you will be able to keep an open mind when settling down in YNC, and this is very important.

Having done all of the above you should be left with whatever you can carry in whatever mode of transport you will be taking to your new life. Bravo!

We will discuss packing your luggage in Chapter 14.

CHAPTER 9

LEAVING LOVED ONES

Happiness is having a large, loving, caring, close-knit family...
in another country.
GEORGE BURNS[1]

Talk to any Sensible Girl who has emigrated and ask what she misses most about home and you're pretty much guaranteed that she will say 'friends and family'. In fact the main thing that holds people back when thinking about emigrating is the prospect of missing loved ones. According to a UK survey,[2] 47 per cent of British women questioned said that 'missing family and friends' was the major reason for not emigrating.

The idea of leaving loved ones behind really seems to preoccupy the girls far more than the guys. See for yourself. Next time you're out with your friends* ask them what they think about emigrating.

---

* In order for this experiment to work, you need to have a both male and female chums present.

When the conversation gets going, it's nearly always the girls who move on to the topic of emotional issues first, 'Oooh no, I couldn't leave my parents/mates/sister behind'. The blokes on the other hand make light of the dilemma by retorting 'I bloody could' and laughing uproariously.

'Women are more dependent on a social network,' point out expat coaches Sabina and Nynke.[3] And this is usually cause for concern when they begin the emigration process. But don't be fooled into thinking that men don't feel a teeny bit worried about saying goodbye too.

According to counselling psychologist Lisa Palmer,[4] 'Women and men find change equally challenging, but it is the women who are socialised to express emotion, to admit to experiencing some form of anxiety and to be "allowed" to be vulnerable. Men on the other hand, are not given the same sort of "permission" and so tend not to discuss the emotional concerns that emigration presents quite as openly as women.'

So, even though it may appear that it is only the Sensible Girls out there who are nervous about leaving their loved ones behind, dig a little deeper and you might find that your big-strong-bear of a boyfriend could actually be a little wobbly jelly inside.

Be gentle.

TELLING PEOPLE YOU'RE LEAVING

The first issue you will need to tackle is when to tell loved ones of your plans. Most of them will probably have a sneaking suspicion of what you've been up to, as emigration plans are tricky to keep under wraps. However, you should only officially announce your plans once you (plus your 'other half', if you own one) are totally happy and confident with your decision. People love you and people will miss you, so you are going to need every ounce of strength to cope with all the 'I wish you weren't leaving-s' and 'don't go-s' that you're going to hear over the next few months. You don't want to lose your nerve.

Where practical, try to tell your loved ones face-to-face. Try to tell friends or family individually so you really talk things through together. Delivering such a surprise announcement to one large group can bring on mass hysteria and scare the living hell out of you.

Tell your parents as soon as possible. If you are an only child, appreciate the consequences of your decision. In simple terms, they are going to miss you. So don't mistake a lack of enthusiasm as a lack of support. If your dad keeps finding reasons for you not to go, it's only because he is worried about you.

If you have brothers and sisters, that certainly doesn't get you off the hook and make things easier for your parents. They are still going to miss you, as are your siblings.

If you have children who are emigrating with you, appreciate that there could be some family members who will be quite upset about your decision. That doesn't mean to say you shouldn't be going, but try to come up with a contingency plan so that Granny and Gramps or Aunty Dotty can see the little ones as often as possible.

If you find your parents are overly enthusiastic about your new decision, be suspicious! They may think a granny flat at the bottom of the garden in YNC is just the solution to their retirement dilemmas. You have been warned...

There will always be a reason to delay your trip, so think carefully about what you do and don't want to accommodate into your timetable. Without wishing to sound heartless, if you wait around for all the weddings, births or birthday parties, you'll never leave. This is your future, your life, so I'm afraid that sometimes you have to be a little bit selfish. Anyway, you can always fly back for the important stuff.

Once you start telling people, be prepared for the floodgates to open. Everyone will be interested, everyone will want to know exactly what you're going to do and everyone will have a good old gossip behind your back. Fair enough. Some may think you're bonkers, some will be jealous and you may even discover a few wannabe escapologists lurking in your midst who have been secretly dreaming about emigrating for years. Who knows, maybe you can inspire a few such lost souls along the way!

Don't worry if you discover 'grey areas' when explaining your plans to everyone. You are still working through everything and will not have a fully functioning, watertight strategy just yet. That's fine and nobody can expect you to have all the answers at this stage. Emigrating is an organic process that grows with every step you take, so have patience.

The important thing to reassure everyone (and yourself) is that there's no such thing as forever. At this early stage you are simply giving it a go, so there's no point in them worrying that you are gone, never to return.

Another hurdle that you and your loved ones must get over is that of distance. For people who are emigrating to Europe, consider the following. You have probably sat in a traffic jam on the M25 longer than it will now take for you to fly home. There is also a strong possibility that you will see some of your friends *more often* once you move abroad than you did when you lived a couple of hours drive away. You will make more of an effort to see them every time you fly back to the UK and they will be keen to come and stay for a cheap holiday abroad. Everyone's a winner. The same mind-set can be applied to anywhere else, really, as the maximum travel time you can notch up is roughly one day's travel. OK, so that's not down the road any more, but it isn't on another planet either. Distance is in the mind as much as on the milometer.

You may also find that, once you've moved overseas, return trips to visit family and friends will involve spending much more quality time with each individual. Whereas before you could pop round for Sunday roast at your mum and dad's and disappear immediately after the washing up was done, now, you will be staying for a long weekend or (if YNC is further afield) a long fortnight. So they're getting you in 'one big lump', rather than having you in evenly distributed 'blobs' throughout the year – if you see what I mean!

PREPARATION

Yes, leaving family and friends behind is the worst aspect of emigrating, but it doesn't all have to be doom and gloom. Lisa, our resident counselling psychologist believes in preparation.[5]

'You can prepare yourself for the inevitable sense of loss that you will have to work through once you emigrate. Talk about how you are going to make contact with each other prior to leaving. For example, will you phone or e-mail? Establishing how you will continue to connect with each other, is affirming the reality that you WILL remain connected, despite geographical distance.'

Maybe plan a holiday or long weekend once you're settled in. Work around someone's birthday or even a Christmas or Easter break. Keeping connected across the miles will help you cope with the changes your friendships will experience in the next few months.

GenXpat author, Margaret Malewski,[6] agrees that the way you say your goodbyes is important, as not only will it give you that obvious 'sense of closure' that is required when moving overseas, but it will also 'lay a good foundation for your long-distance relationships' and allow you to fully concentrate on settling in once you arrive in YNC rather than being distracted by social commitments back in Blighty.

Improved long-distance connections could be viewed as another reason for rising emigration figures. It's never been so easy to keep in contact with loved ones back home. You can write a letter, e-mail, chat on the mobile or landline, text, send photos and movies, MSN, Twitter, upload your photo-story on to Facebook or chat into the small hours for free on Skype.

It is important to select the method of communication that best suits your loved ones back home. For example, now that I live in Australia, I e-mail a particular office-based friend back in London pretty much every day. We have a proper conversation, just like we would if we were down the road from each other. I have another, equally well-loved friend who works in the film industry who can't readily access a computer. I don't speak to her for a couple of months and then, out of the blue, she'll phone me for a good old gossip (usually at around 4am because she's forgotten the time difference!). Both are great friends and both require completely different methods of staying in touch. So talk to loved ones and work out whether people like Aunty Dotty need a quick lesson on e-mail or whether they would prefer a good old-fashioned letter!

Likewise, cheaper travel means that you can now visit loved ones on a far more regular basis. Granted you won't be nipping out with mates for a spontaneous Friday knees-up, but they can still be there for you. Real friends don't just disappear, even if you won't be seeing them quite as much as you used to. They will always be there for you, no matter where you go and live. Ask any Sensible Girl living abroad what it is like to visit family and friends in the UK and the unanimous response will be 'It's like I never left!'

And that's what it will always be like with really good friends and family. The truth is that if you are happy and excited about the decision you have made, then everyone else will be pleased for you. Sure, you are going to miss everyone and the chances are that you will get homesick, but accept this, as it's only natural and try not to worry about it (we will discuss homesickness at great length later in the book).

Anyway, you have far more important things to be planning – like your leaving party, for starters!

LEAVING PARTY ETIQUETTE

You must have a fabulous leaving do. It's not optional; it's essential.

Just remember not to get too preoccupied with party planning and forget all of your other spinning plates. There's a lot to think about, so consult that calendar.

HOSTING A DIVINE DEPARTING 'DO'
TOP TIPS FOR YOUR LEAVING PARTY

1. Try hinting to your friends about having a 'surprise!' leaving party, then you can relinquish all responsibilities and get on with the other stuff. Just make sure you also hint about the venue, invite list, dress code, decor, drinks menu, canapés, lighting, etc.!

2. Avoid having too many leaving parties, such as:
   * one for work;
   * one for old friends;
   * one for family;
   * one for partner's friends and family;
   * one for friends who live in another part of the country...

   You have too much to do and not enough new outfits (remember the saving plan). Plus you will end up feeling and looking exhausted before you even get out of the country.

3. To avoid disappointment, plan well in advance. Send out proper invites so everyone can put the date in their diary.

4. Do not hold your leaving party the day before you depart – for many obvious reasons, all of which contain the word 'sick'.

5. Try dropping the occasional hint about what you want for a leaving present. Remember you've just cleared the clutter out of your life and want to be able to carry the present in your luggage to YNC, so the crystal Martini jug you've been eyeing up in Selfridges is probably not the way to go this time!

6. BUY A FABULOUS NEW DRESS...forget the savings plan, just this once!

7. Don't forget to take your camera, don't forget to take it out of your bag at least once at the party and take some photos and don't forget to put it back into your bag at the end of the night and take it home with you. Simple now; so much more complicated after a few mojitos.

8. If you have access to some kind of video camera, try to get everyone to record messages for you throughout the night. Replaying the footage once you're abroad and watching your friends drunkenly declare their undying love for you while supping on a cocktail, will help you deal with all those nasty bouts of homesickness once you're in YNC.

9. Wear waterproof mascara and carry plenty of tissues.

CHAPTER 10

TRAVEL ARRANGEMENTS

Everywhere is within walking distance, if you have the time.
STEVEN WRIGHT[1]

The rollercoaster ride is well under way and you are steadily crossing things off your checklists. In fact, things are progressing quite nicely.

Amidst this controlled mayhem you will have a moment of clarity. You will see exactly how far you've come and know precisely what is left to be done. Once you know this, you will be able to put a timescale on everything and if you haven't already got a leaving date in your calendar...you have now!

It's time to make that final commitment to reaching YNC and book your ticket.

Some of you will be skipping over (or under) the Channel to Continental pastures new, but the majority of you will be winging your way further overseas. Either way, the end result of this decision is a little piece of paper with a date and time on it!

Like it or not, you now officially have a deadline to work towards. Properties need to be vacated, belongings packed, jobs left and loved ones kissed goodbye. The thought of which could leave you...

Looking like this: or like this:

If you're freaking out, try to stay calm: nothing has actually changed...you've just got a clearer timescale, that's all. If you have sensibly worked through your schedule (when to move out of your home, storage collection, timings, job resignation, etc.) and allowed for the odd hiccup along the way, everything will be fine.

It's really rather exciting.

✈

FABULOUS FLIGHT BOOKING TIPS

- Try to save an extra few pounds so that you can take a well-earned holiday en route to YNC, even if it's just for a couple of days. You deserve it. Your stress levels have been steadily rising, so by the time you step on that plane, you will be gagging for a sun lounger and a copy of *Hello!* magazine.

- If you are a little nervous about your emigration, an open-ended return ticket can be another security blanket option. More often than not, the price difference between a single and a return is minimal, especially for longer-haul flights. Shop around and see what's on offer. If you decide to opt for this type of ticket, make sure you don't forget your return date and let the ticket expire. A good way of avoiding this is to book the approximate date you think you'd like to pop back to Blighty,* and give this date to your parents. They will not let you forget it!
- Some airlines have special offers for people who are emigrating. Such as a one-way ticket with anything up to a double luggage allowance (which can be an absolute godsend). You will be able to find out about these offers through any good flight centre, emigration agent or travel agent, or by contacting the airline direct. But be warned, Expat Forums reveal that there can be inconsistency in the agreement and once you begin your travels, other airline staff claim no knowledge of the special offer (and you get stung!). So make sure you get the luggage allowance confirmed in writing when making the booking.
- Some airlines offer a discounted excess rate if you pre-pay online. Others may offer extra options if you're carrying specific sporting equipment over (giving you an added weight allowance). Essentially, any trick that can save you a few quid is worth it!

---

* In order for this fabulous booking tip to be of use, please make sure the ticket you book has a changeable return date!

- Think ahead when deciding which airline to use and make sure they are affiliated with some kind of Airmiles scheme. You may as well fly with the same company each time you travel and rack up a few bonuses in the process. And don't forget to enquire about expiry dates when working out which company to go for.
- Get to know your favoured airline company's schedule. Airlines will often have sales during off-peak times when flights can be a lot cheaper. If you can get the timing right, you may save yourself a few quid. A Sensible Girl should already know that you should avoid emigrating on a half-term or summer bank holiday weekend!
- A lot of airlines let you select your seat online and some will even take emergency exit seat booking requests when you purchase the ticket. This has absolutely sod all to do with emigrating...but everything to do with comfort. Remember this now and you will enjoy a thrombosis-free flight later.
- Just because you have squirrelled away all of your money over the last few months, it does not mean that you should even consider treating yourself and going business class – especially when there is always the chance of the elusive upgrade to aim for.

SENSIBLE STATS
*TOP TEN EMIGRATION DESTINATIONS FOR SENSIBLE GIRLS
AND THEIR FLIGHT TIMES FROM THE UK*
(i.e. How far from 'home' you're REALLY going to be)[2]

The Sensible Girl's Top Ten Emigration Destinations	Time it takes to fly from Heathrow Airport
1 AUSTRALIA	Perth: 19 hours 30 minutes Sydney: 22 hours Melbourne: 22 hours 30 minutes Brisbane: 23 hours 30 minutes
2 SPAIN	Barcelona: 2 hours Madrid: 2 hours 20 minutes
3 FRANCE	Paris: 1 hour
4 NEW ZEALAND	Auckland: 25 hours Wellington: 29 hours Christchurch: 30 hours
5 USA	New York: 7 hours 30 minutes Miami: 9 hours 45 minutes Seattle: 9 hours 45 minutes San Francisco: 11 hours
6 GERMANY	Berlin: 1 hour 45 minutes
7 CANADA	Montréal: 7 hours 20 minutes Toronto: 8 hours Vancouver: 9 hours 45 minutes
8 THAILAND	Bangkok: 12 hours
9 UNITED ARAB EMIRATES (UAE)	Abu Dhabi/Dubai: 7 hours
10 NETHERLANDS	Amsterdam: 1 hour 25 minutes

INSURANCE

Make sure you take out a good comprehensive insurance policy that is appropriate to your circumstances.

Unless you're lucky, you will not be moving straight into a secure property of your own. You will either be travelling around, staying with friends or living in temporary/holiday accommodation for the first few weeks, so you need to be fully covered if anything disastrous happens.

You don't necessarily need to cover yourself for a long period of time, just until you can set up a decent insurance policy in YNC.

Beware of bog-standard holiday insurance options as they often require a return flight date at the end of the period for which you want to cover yourself. This would mean that you would have to return to the UK if you needed to make a claim – costly and a complete waste of your time. You require something a bit more flexible and there are insurance policies out there specifically tailored to people who are emigrating.

When reading the fine print, check what the maximum pay-out is for individual items. The nature of your trip means that you will probably be carrying a lot of valuable stuff on your way out (your jewellery, your iPod, your Miu-Miu pumps), so you need to be sufficiently covered in case of any mishaps.

Depending on your circumstances, taking out private medical insurance could be a pre-requisite of the visa application, especially if you are a Sensible Senior and retiring abroad. Getting the appropriate cover is of the utmost importance, so if in any doubt, ask an emigration expert who can point you in the right direction.

You also have the emigration 'safety net option' of paying for Repatriation Insurance, which, for the worriers out there, allows the holder to return to the UK (all expenses paid) if there is some kind of emergency. Most Sensible Girls might feel this is a bit excessive, but if, for example, you have a poorly relative who is threatening to get poorlier, this could be a worthwhile investment.

If you are dealing with an emigration agency, they might be able to recommend a tried-and-trusted policy. And, as always, make sure you read the small print and stick with a reputable company.

ACCOMMODATION BOOKING

If you are not lucky enough to be heading straight into the welcoming bosom of a close (or distant) friend or relative, you will need to book accommodation for your arrival, even if it's only for the first couple of weeks before you find a rental property.

If you have the cash, by all means treat yourself to a dose of luxury for the first couple of days and go for the five-star boutique option with infinity rooftop swimming pool. Just remember that you can't stay somewhere posh for too long – as this is not a holiday!

Another option is booking holiday rental accommodation, which offers you short-term flexibility without the hotel price tag. These can be great, but make sure you know exactly where they are, as you might need something a bit more central than the rustic log cabin that's advertised. Also make sure they have all the facilities that you need (phone, broadband, fax) to assist in your quest for settling down.

If you are completely clueless about YNC's accommodation situation, maybe you should seek the services a relocation agent (already bigged-up in Chapter 7) as one of their primary functions is 'meeting and greeting' emigration virgins when they land in their new country to delivering them safely to their lodgings.

While you are reading this in the comfort of your own country, it might seem a little unnecessary. But remember, when you are in the arrivals lounge of YNC, you are going to be tired, emotional, stressed and a teensy bit clueless about where to go, so a smiley person holding up your name on a piece of cardboard might be the way to go.

CHAPTER 11

FOURTEEN DAYS AND COUNTING...

Obstacles are those frightful things you see when you take your eyes off your goal.
HENRY FORD[1]

Well, you're completely knackered and you feel like you might have to punch someone – but that's OK because you're almost there! Those goalposts are finally looming into view and you're sizing up for the final kick.

Before you do, make sure that all of your loose ends are tied up. Use the following checklists so you don't forget anything.

WORK STUFF

• If you haven't given up work already, you should be just about to.	
• You should have a glowing reference from your boss in duplicate.	
• You should have opened a Hotmail/Yahoo/bloody-big-banana e-mail account and moved all of your personal e-mail addresses into its address book, including helpful work contacts (you never know what favours you'll need once you've reached YNC).	
• You should have let everyone know your new e-mail address.	
• You should have hidden any work that you couldn't be bothered to finish, so that it will not be discovered until you have left.	✓

HOUSE STUFF

• If you are renting out your property you should have signed a contract and be very close to having a tenant in place (if they're not already).	
• If you are selling your property, you should have pretty much 'done the deal' or be all lined up to carry on proceedings from overseas.	

• If you are moving out of your parents' house, your father is forbidden from making 'renting your room out' gags until you have left the country.	✓
• You should have already sorted out a place to stay in the interim before leaving the UK.	

PAPERWORK STUFF

• All your paperwork should be up to date and in order.	
• Your box file should be sorted and your Box Guardian should have been given a guided tour so they can find everything if required.	
• Tickets, passports, etc., should be stored safely AWAY from anything that is about to be taken into storage.	

STUFF STUFF

• You should have sold, binned and burnt your disposable belongings and now be experiencing Possession Nirvana.	
• If you are storing or shipping stuff, it should be packed away already...or about to be.	
• If you are stashing stuff at a friend's or relative's house, they should be aware of it.	

Aside from tying up those last few fiddly loose ends, there is another good reason for having time to spare before you leave... so you can go out and have some fun! You are going away indefinitely, so you want your lasting memories of home to be wonderful! If you have been a good, Sensible Girl, you will now have a healthy bank account and a super-friendly bank manager, which means you are ready to enjoy The Holy Trinity:

Socialising / Shopping / Sprucing

SOCIALISING: YOUR SOCIAL WHIRL

Never in all your life have you been in such demand. You're considering hiring a personal publicist and diary organiser, not to mention someone to answer your phone. Enjoy all the attention. Enjoy all of your family and friends company. Enjoy being a full-time social butterfly!

Go and see everyone. Not just your usual friends, but the ones who live out of town, old schoolfriends, university mates and travelling chums – basically, anyone who you kept meaning to visit, but didn't quite get round to. This also includes all relatives who haven't seen you since you were knee high to a Brownie. Whether it's for a quick cup of tea or a night on the town, they will all really appreciate you dropping by and, in the months ahead, you'll really appreciate that you did.

Go to your favourite restaurants, bars, cinemas, art galleries, museums and so on. Even if an afternoon tucked up on the sofa watching DVDs seems more appealing, get up and get out! You are going to miss all of these things once you leave them behind. Eat your favourite meals, drink your favourite drinks – indulge yourself.

SHOPPING: YOUR RETAIL THERAPY

This only applies if you have saved enough money and have not been 'proper shopping' for the last few months.

Go out and treat yourself. But don't forget that these purchases will have to fit into your luggage. Do it on a weekday when marauding teenagers and the like are not going to get in your way. You will also find that a supportive shopping buddy and a boozy lunch will enhance the whole experience.

We've already established that it is essential to buy a new party outfit for your leaving do.

Stock up on Essential English Items (EEIs). These are things that you will not be able to buy in YNC, such as M&S undies, Topshop tops, Marmite, Monster Munch, a quarter of rhubarb and custards...whatever shakes your tree (and isn't going to bother passport control or customs).

Don't panic-buy and find you can't fit everything into your luggage, as there are plenty of expat websites knocking around that will deliver such delicacies once you have settled in YNC. Limiting yourself to three family packs of PG Tips will probably be enough to keep you going...for the time being anyway.

SPRUCING: YOUR BEAUTY BONANZA

Whether you're after a trim, a blow dry, or a semi-demi-wave-deep-conditioning-full-head-of-highlights, make a final date with your hairdresser. After all, you don't know how long it will be before your next appointment.

A Sensible Girl knows that it is *very* important to find a decent hairstylist in Their New Country. If you rush your search, bad choices can be made and things can go terribly wrong. Your beautiful layered locks can be transformed into a bleached mullet in a matter of snips, the results of which can be cataclysmic and prevent any hope of future happiness...well, at least until things grow out. Apply the same rule to manicurists, pedicurists, masseurs, waxers (especially waxers!), tanning salons, and so on.

Obviously try to get everything 'done' the day before your glamorous leaving party. Note that your beauty bonanza should be done on a separate date to your shopping spree. There are not enough hours in one day for the two to be effectively enjoyed simultaneously.

BITS AND BOBS
Here are a few important (and not so important) things to occupy your two-week countdown.

ADDRESS BOOK UPDATE
Don't just concentrate on getting all of your friends' and family's contact details. You will need to make sure that you have phone numbers and e-mail addresses for a few other less scintillating people:

> * your bank (and card protection scheme emergency number);
> * your doctor, orthodontist, reflexologist, psychoanalyst...just in case;
> * your rental agency/storage company/quarantine agent, etc.

Be sure to take a number that will work when dialled from outside the UK as freephone numbers often don't work abroad. Even better, try to get numbers that directly put you through to a real person, otherwise you'll be spending 45 minutes pressing 'the star key twice' or 'the hash key once' before you are put through to a human being.

Also feel free to include PIN numbers and passwords, although hide them within other phone numbers for added security.

CHANGE OF ADDRESS
Change all bank accounts, mailing lists, doctor's surgery records, etc., to a new UK contact address, preferably to that of the Box Guardian (your mum?). Remember, it is polite to warn that person that they are about to receive all of your future bank

statements, sample sale notifications and smear test reminders from now on.

Alternatively, the Royal Mail offers redirection services for up to two years. You will have to pay for this facility and you will obviously need a fixed address in YNC for them to forward your mail to. So this option is only for the lucky girls who have a permanent address (or friends and family who have one) ready and waiting for them overseas.

CASH THINGS IN

Whether it's your annual travel card or a platinum gym pass, your TV licence, RAC membership or tax disc, check how long they're valid for and claim any refunds where possible. You might be surprised how much money you can get back.

CERTIFIED COPIES

Depending what personal documentation you are taking with you (and I would strongly suggest leaving some of it in a safe UK place until you are more settled), it is a sensible plan to take a few certified copies of paperwork, such as birth certificates, divorce papers, degree certificates, etc., with you. You might want to get married or simply apply for a new job in YNC and these pieces of paper will make your life *so* much easier.

DIRECT DEBITS

Make sure all direct debits have been properly cancelled now that you have moved out of your property. Pay off all credit cards and make sure your bank knows you will suddenly be using them in a foreign country (as they sometimes freeze accounts if your spending pattern changes). Cancel standing orders and subscriptions and make sure you have an up-to-date bank statement for each account that you are leaving behind.

GUIDEBOOKS

Now you should have been merrily referencing your CSE book for some time now, but what if you're moving somewhere a bit 'left of centre' that isn't lucky enough to have its very own emigrating guidebook? Grab a *Lonely Planet* or *Rough Guide* for the region. Good travel guides can still offer loads of helpful information that you're going to be thankful for, even if they can't advise you on the specifics of settling down.

MOBILE PHONE

You may plan to buy a mobile phone in YNC, but try to make sure that you can use your UK mobile there too. That way you're guaranteed that nobody from your 'old life' will lose touch with you if they still only have your old number. It will also mean that you only need to buy the SIM card once out there rather than purchase another phone.*

Consider using a 'pay as you go' option to avoid a sterling invoice being raised each month (which will just be a pain in the backside to pay from YNC). Stock up on credit before you leave and this should tide you over before you get your new phone (and remember that unused SIM cards will eventually expire – so check dates).

Depending on your phone's technical capabilities (and yours), either get a phone shop to print off a list of all your mobile's stored phone numbers or download them on to your computer and keep a copy in your box file (while making sure your address book is fully up to date). While it may feel like you're being totally overprotective of your phone numbers, you're not. We rarely know phone numbers off by heart these days, so if you lose your

---

* So long as your mobile phone hasn't got a lock on it that prevents use outside the UK. Check first.

mobile abroad (and that's the only place you have people's contact details stored), it would be a complete nightmare and could make it very difficult to get hold of some of your more distant friends again.

MUSIC

If you have an iPod or mp3 player, organise the soundtrack for your emigration!

If you are a techno-scaredy-cat, bin your plastic CD covers. Pack the discs and paper inserts in one of those ugly CD travel cases. Then buy cheap, new plastic cases at the other end and free up a huge amount of valuable space in your luggage.

If you are stuck in the 80s and still have cassettes, you might want to invest in some 21st-century technology in duty free!

PASSPORT DETAILS

If you haven't ever bothered filling out next of kin details in your passport (technically known as 'the back bit'), do so before you leave.

PASSPORT PHOTOGRAPHS

These are bound to come in handy for all the new ID you will be applying for upon arrival in YNC. Try to time your visit to a photo booth to just after your beauty bonanza!

PURSE CLEAROUT

There are two types of purses in a Sensible Girl's handbag: the petite, gorgeous, but rather useless variety, which holds only a few coins and a TicTac; and the huge, leather colossus that weighs a ton and can barely be closed.

What I'm talking about here is the latter. The one that is currently stuffed with 'hole in the wall' statements, expired coffee shop loyalty cards, receipts that date back to the last century –

and not much cash! Either way, you don't need your Blockbuster membership card and all that other purse detritus where you're heading, so bin it or box file it.

The same goes for key rings. Taking the spare set of your sister's house keys to YNC is not going to help anyone. Give them back.

SAMPLE SEIZING

If you are buying any posh toiletries to take over to YNC, see if you can get a few samples thrown in for good measure, as these will be ideal to carry in your hand luggage, now that airlines have imposed stricter size limitations.

PRESENT BUYING

Buy a nice pressie for your Box Guardian, Post Opener, Stuff Storer, Travel Adviser, and Agony Aunt, who all probably go by the name of Mum or Dad! Don't forget to say a heartfelt thank-you to everyone who has helped over the last few months. They have been life-savers and you probably couldn't have done it without them!

CHAPTER 12

PRE-EMIGRATING AILMENTS

- What state do you want to live in?
- Denial
...Isn't that in Egypt?
ANON

Even the most sensible Sensible Girls can lose it sometimes and when you're in the later throes of leaving the UK and heading for YNC, your stress levels can reach dizzying heights. Everything is happening (or not happening) at the same time and you've noticed a big black cloud hovering just over your head that has begun to follow you around.

Well, they say that identifying the problem is half the solution, so here are a few pre-emigrating disorders (and their cures) that might help you calm down and get a grip before leaving Blighty.

SCHIZOPHRENIA

Symptoms   You want to go.
You don't want to go.
You want to go.
You don't want to go.

Sound familiar?

Life-as-you-knew-it ceased to exist when you signed up for Emigrating Membership, but quite frankly that plain Jane existence you ditched is starting to look like a rather comfy alternative to this madness! Couldn't you just pretend that your visa application was rejected and forget the whole thing? Tell everyone that YNC now only gives working visas to pastry chefs and loo cleaners and go and hide under your bed (or in the space where you once had a bed, now that it's gone into bloody storage).

But then again, maybe you DO want to give it a go!

Cure   Counselling psychologist Lisa Palmer[1] explains that feeling like an emotional yo-yo in the run-up to your emigration is standard procedure:

'Self-doubt is normal and to be expected, given the experience of impending change. But it's when self-doubt completely overwhelms and immobilises you that it becomes an issue.

'The feelings associated with self-doubt are often related to anxiety and fear. Fear is a protective mechanism for survival in new environments; in fact it's not a bad thing at all. It may be helpful to explore this fear within yourself. Sometimes, to literally ask yourself "what is the greatest fear I have about situation X" puts in perspective what the specific issue worrying you might be.'

So what is it that's freaking you out? Think about key issues that are worrying you and work them through rationally with a sensible friend. There will always be some kind of solution!

And if that doesn't work, dig out that Wish List you wrote all those months ago and remind yourself WHY you are doing this.

PSYCHOTIC FREAK OUT

Symptoms   If stress were an Olympic sport, you'd be snivelling on the podium with a gold medal dangling round your neck. Even your local newsagent running out of Biscuit Boosts triggers a life-threatening heart palpitation these days and you're so uptight a pint of Rescue Remedy isn't going to calm you down. Let the psychosis begin...

Cure   Fear, insecurity, lack of confidence, self-doubt...all of these nasty little gremlins are rearing their ugly heads at the moment and trying to trip you up. Just keep hanging on. I know it's a hell of a ride but the rollercoaster will finish looping the loop when you board that plane, and then things should calm down for a while.

According to life coach Lesley Sumner,[2] it's all about acceptance:

'Accept that it's GOING to happen...and that you WANT it to happen. Accept that there is no real way round it and just be brave, steadfast and keep going, knowing that this chaos WILL come to an end.'

You're doing BRILLIANTLY.

What you need is some Time Out. A boozy night with the girls...and just don't mention the 'E' word.

RSI

Symptoms   Having averaged approx 23.5 hours of Internet research per day, your once opposable thumbs have developed rigor mortis and your poor, blistered fingers look like a bunch of well-manicured bananas.

Cure   Sit up straight, uncross your legs, wiggle your fingers, then go outside and get some fresh air, for goodness sake!

Limit that Internet interaction to a sensible amount of hours per day!

'WHAT IF' INFECTION

Symptoms   What if you hate it?

What if you don't make any friends and end up living alone in a house full of stray cats that smells of wee?

What if you never manage to pick up the language and have to work as a mute shelf stacker for all eternity?

What if your family and friends forget all about you and the space that you once occupied closes up...FOREVER?

Cure   OK...

What if you love it?

What if you make brilliant, lifelong friends?

What if you pick up the language easily once you're there?

What if you stop being such a drama queen and get on with it!

SPANNERITIS

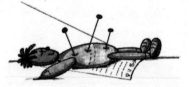

Symptoms   The path to emigration happiness is long and rarely smooth – but that doesn't make it any less annoying when some horrid person throws a big fat spanner in the works at the eleventh hour.

Whether it's the bollocksy immigration bureau in YNC who's just changed its points criteria at the last minute or that nasty, evil couple who were meant to buy your house but have 'changed their minds', grrrrr...

Cure   Anger management.

Feel free to scream loud obscenities in the privacy of your own home or make voodoo dolls of anyone who has 'wronged' you.

But, most of all, put it down to experience and move on!

MORBID RELATIVES

Symptoms   Granny used to say: 'I might be dead before you come and visit again' – and that was when you lived down the road. Now that she knows of your intentions to live 'somewhere foreign', she's started dishing out her knick-knacks and reminding you what Cliff Richard song she wants played at her funeral. Good grief!

Cure   Sensible Psychologist Lisa[3] gets straight to the point:

'Emotional blackmail occurs when one party [that's Granny!], via the use of victimisation or pity, incites guilt and doubt in the other party [that's you].

'It's a very effective, back-handed use of power and control where the person on the receiving end can experience guilt, shame and a sense of unease in response to their emigration intentions. It is important to empathise with the person [that's Granny again!] and appreciate the impact that your departure will have on them. But you must remain firm and resolute, restating the importance of your own decision.'

It's all about keeping the doors of communication open and listening to each other. Just try to ignore her jibes. Grannies were never known for their subtlety at the best of times. Give her a hug and tell her that you'll be back to visit before she can say 'Devil Woman'.

And put those knick-knacks back where they came from.

FRIENDS WHO TURN A BIT WEIRD

Symptoms   You've told friends and family about your emigrating intentions, and on the whole everyone is thrilled for you. But there's a rogue friend or relative who has taken your emigration on board... and gone all weird.

'Weird friend' symptoms can include snappiness, sullenness, sarcasm, snideyness or just simply ignoring you (and the fact that you're emigrating) and side effects can range from irritation to emotional devastation (depending on the quality of the friend in question).

Cure

Surprisingly, this is a fairly common emigrating ailment, and one that always catches people unawares.

Even through the decision to move to another country is 'pure genius' as far as you're concerned, it's not the be-all and end-all of everyone else's lives. To others, it can dredge up feelings of jealousy or desertion, or they may simply feel that your plans are a personal slur against the friendship. They may feel inadequate because they don't have the courage to do something as 'daring' as you. Or they may feel annoyed because you're talking about moving to YNC instead of acknowledging the important issues in their life (see You're So Boring, page 185).

In order to eradicate all traces of weirdness, you will have to remove your emigrating ego and delve a little deeper to see why your mate is behaving the way they are. The only way to cure any friends acting in this way is to talk to them and find out what is really bothering them.

And if the symptoms continue – smile, and rise above it!

PATIENCE DEFICIENCY

Symptoms You've been waiting for 14 months, two weeks and three days and you STILL haven't heard about your visa application. BORED NOW! Have they lost it? Has it dropped down the back of some useless pen pusher's desk? Have they all died and gone to Foreign Embassy Heaven? What the hell's going on?

Cure By all means check in with your immigration agent once in a while, but do not pester them or anyone else who is involved with your application. These people hold your future in their in-tray and you don't want to piss them off by making a nuisance of yourself. You might feel like your patience is running out, but I'm afraid you'll have to put up with it, because there is no real cure for this one.

TELEPHONUS GARGANTUOUS

Symptoms Bloody Nora!
So you've made a few long-distance phone calls recently, but if you'd known it was going to cost 'that much' you'd have booked a first class flight and gone there in person...via St Kitts!

Cure If you do find that you have to make international phone calls, invest in a cheap rate pre-paid phone card. Using a PIN code and a local-rate phone number, you can make all of your calls and save yourself a wad of cash.

'OH MY GOD – YOU'RE SO BORING'

Symptoms   You know the one about the sweet young girl who started to arrange her wedding? She got a bit carried away and eventually all she could talk about was bridal bouquets, dress swatches and chair covers.

Within six short months she had morphed from maiden to monster, bored all her friends into hiding and was re-named Bridezilla!

Ahem...

Cure   OK, so you're talking about visa applications, flight times and shipping insurance, but it's the same principle.

Your friends love you dearly – but if you don't change the record there could be a few empty seats at your leaving do. I know it might not seem plausible, but there is more to life than your Denby dinner set reaching Dubai in one piece – so put a sock in it and talk about the weather instead!

CHAPTER 14

PACKING

No pressure...no diamonds.
MARY CASE[1]

When you started reading this book, you were going about your daily business, leading a normal life, living in a house full of 'stuff'. Now, after all your hard work, everything you are left with should fit into your suitcase. Pretty impressive! (We'll overlook the fact that your shipping container is chocka-block and your parents' attic is about to collapse.)

The chances are you will need to start packing well in advance of your actual departure date, as you will be moving out of your home and in with either family or friends in the run-up to your departure. If so, re-pack everything the day before you actually leave the country as there are bound to be a few things that you *don't* need– like one battered, party dress with a big fat wine stain down the front, for starters!

Before you can pack anything you must work out what you are going to travel in.

AIRPORT OUTFIT

'You don't have to lose all sense of style and wear your worst outfit just because you're flying,' warns fashion director of *Company* magazine, Oonagh Brennan.[2] 'You're not ill, so do not go for the oversized baggy T-shirt and elasticated tracky-bottoms option.'

Naturally, it is of the utmost importance that you leave loved ones with a lingering memory of how gorgeous you always look. So planning your airport outfit well in advance is a good idea. Referencing a few well-chosen paparazzi shots has been known to help illustrate what's hot in 'airline couture', so feel free to stock up on trashy pap mags (like you needed an excuse!).

'Be warm and layer up, as planes can be chilly,' suggests Oonagh, 'especially if you are travelling between climates and want to walk into the arrivals lounge wearing something summery. Remember that tights and boots can be removed en route and replaced with sandals or flip-flops...and a pair of Uggs can save the day, whatever the weather.'

You must take style, comfort and practicality into consideration. Remember that the more you can wear, the less you need to pack. It's all about layering, but without looking like the Michelin woman. Coats and bulky jumpers will all make good cushions, while pashminas/shawls double as blankets. Try to keep a sense of style when piling on those layers, for there is one thing that a Sensible Girl never misses...

...the opportunity of an upgrade!

Emigrating is stressful enough – without facing the prospect of a showdown at the check-in desk, so make sure you pack sensibly.

'Knowing what you can and cannot take on board, as well as how much you can carry, can make all the difference to your journey,' advises British Airways.[3] 'Be prepared, plan ahead and get your journey off to a good start.'

So, let's start off with the big boys.

THE BIG BAGS
(CHECKED-IN LUGGAGE THAT WILL GO IN THE HOLD)

WEIGHT/SIZE
First of all, check with your airline to find out what your maximum weight allowance is for luggage that will be placed in

the hold. The standard free allowance for an Economy ticket is usually between 20kg and 23kg and the absolute maximum allowance for any single piece of baggage is 32kg (for which you will probably have to pay for the excess). And if you want to get down to specifics, measurements are usually around the 90cm × 75cm × 43xm.[4]

Business class and first class will obviously have higher limits (around 30–40kg), *but* if you do upgrade on the spot (either by paying upfront, or sweet-talking the attendant), you will not automatically get those extra weight benefits (thanks to the short notice of the upgrade).

As previously mentioned, if you have some kind of sporting equipment that you will be taking with you (skis, surfboard, bicycle, etc.), this will need to have been cleared with the airline rather than just rocking up with it – and you may have to pay a small fee upfront.

If you find that you are over your limit, stay positive. You can sometimes be lucky and find yourself on a half-empty flight with a friendly check-in attendant who is sympathetic to your cause. So if you know that you are slightly 'overweight', don't march up to the counter ready to pick a fight, as that will just get the attendant's back up.

Smile and explain the situation.

Smile a bit more and if they do start making noises that you will have to pay for excess luggage, ask if there is someone else you can speak to...but keep on smiling!

Remember: while you can try to negotiate don't get too carried away as their word is final.

SPECIFICS

- **Pack the sensible stuff.** You're not going backpacking this time, so don't forget to pack smart outfits, job interview apparel and work clothes (not just a sarong and flip-flops).

- **Pack clothing for all climates** (not just T-shirts and bikinis as you will be living in YNC through all the seasons).

- **Pack practical, sports and outdoor clothing** (not just the fabulous stuff).

- **Pack a decent towel** (not just the ropey beach one with a smiley whale on it).

- **Pack adaptors for any electrical appliances you're taking with you.** Even if you intend to change the plugs once you settle in YNC, you won't do it immediately. Trust me, if you have an emergency-hair-straightening-moment you don't want to be faffing around with a screwdriver for 15 minutes!

- **BUT...don't pack too many electrical appliances.** Depending on your destination, you can always re-buy the cheaper items out there if you are pushed for space!

- **Pack a modest amount of toiletries**. Girls aren't very good at this. But unless you are emigrating to a really remote place (in which case go for your life and pack the lot), take travel-sized toiletries. You can always buy a sackful of potions and lotions once you're out there, but you don't want to do it now and have to pay for excess baggage in the process.

Many essential grooming products are available internationally these days, so it's highly likely that you will still be able to find your favourite anti-static, de-frizz hair serum in YNC. The only difference being that if you're moving somewhere a bit exotic, it might be called 'Bumm' or 'Whiffy Waa' instead – but you can live with that.

- **Pack a modest amount of drugs**. Obviously *not* the illegal sort. While you'll still be able to get most of your everyday medications in YNC, it's never sensible to stray too far away from a packet of painkillers. So pack a few first aid goodies in your wash bag. Don't forget to stock up on any prescriptive medication (the Pill, for example) as it may take a while for you to work out where you'll be getting your next batch from.

- **Pack a sensible selection of smalls**. Girls' underwear drawers are all the same. At the front of the drawers are the comfortable bras and pants you wear on a daily basis, while taking up approximately 75 per cent of drawer space are lingerie items that no longer see the light of day (or night!). Usually taking the form of two rubber bands tacked together with lace, these saucy smalls have to go and there is only one appropriate place to stash them – the bin! And while you're there,

> throw out any other offending underwear. If they're old, grey or baggy...haven't we discussed these already? Do the male population a favour and get rid of them!

IDENTIFICATION

As we've already established, you're carrying some very important cargo on this trip – what boils down to all your worldly belongings (other than what is in storage). So you don't want things getting lost.

Whether you're staying with loved ones or bunking up in a cheap motel in YNC, label everything with your new contact details (mobile phone numbers and e-mail addresses are handy if you're still a little unsure of physical addresses).

Unless you have bespoke psychedelic luggage, you'll need to try to make your suitcases stand out from everyone else's on the carousel. So buy a bright luggage strap or tie a short piece of brightly coloured ribbon securely round one of your handles. Anything to stand out.

THE LITTLE BAGS (HAND LUGGAGE)

Thanks to tightened airport security, hand baggage restrictions have been made even stricter so Rule Number One is; **if there is**

anything you are unsure of, check with your airline. Most airlines have pretty comprehensive websites with all the information you need, so log on and learn.

WEIGHT/SIZE
Most well-travelled Sensible Girls know that there are two types of people on this planet – the ones who obey the hand luggage rule and the ones who arrive at the departures gate dragging a super-sized-wheelie case, capable of housing a small teenager. These irritating people then require the assistance of three flight attendants to hoist their ridiculously large bag into the overhead lockers, before flopping down next to you and stealing your armrest.

But being good Sensible Girls – we're not like that, are we?!

Airlines usually impose a 5kg hand luggage weight limit and the bag in question is required to be of a certain dimension (something along the lines of 56cm x 45cm x 25cm).[5] You will usually be allowed to also carry a handbag/laptop bag as well – but it is always safe to check how strict your airline's hand luggage policies are.

But once you are clear on your allowances, make sure you use your hand luggage quota, as there's no point struggling to fit everything in your main luggage, while ignoring the opportunity to squish a few more extra items in your carry-on.

BANNED ITEMS
As if not having easy access to your trusty tweezers wasn't cause for alarm, now you are faced with the prospect of having your bumper bottle of Keihl's moisturiser confiscated before boarding the plane. Thanks to heightened airport security, banned items now include liquid containers housing anything over 100ml (even if the container is not full). SO downsize your carry-on

cosmetics and take miniatures of everything you need for the flight in a clear plastic bag.

OTHER HANDY HINTS FOR YOUR 'LITTLE BAG' PACKING

• **Don't forget to pack this book in your hand luggage**. You are going to need it on the plane.
• **Use the 'Russian doll technique'**. In order to take as many bags as possible. Pack a bag, within a bag, within a bag, within a...you get the idea!
• **Pack electronics carefully**. Yes, so long as they can be put through the X-ray machine and don't exceed your hand luggage quota, you can carry your electronics with you. So whether it's your iPod, digital camera, mobile, BlackBerry® or laptop, try and pack them in your carry-on. But feel free to shove all adapters, chargers (except your mobile charger – in case of emergencies) and connecting leads in your 'big case' otherwise you'll look like you've just robbed Dixons.
• **Keep all of your important paperwork on you**. Including any key emigration documents, bank details as well as any computer discs, USB's or what not, that you will be travelling with.
• **Light reading**. Pack a large selection of UK glossy fashion magazines (to be purchased at the airport).

- **Emotional emergency**. Don't leave for the airport without a family pack of travel tissues and waterproof mascara.

- **Study your paparazzi shots**. After extensive research into 'airline couture' you will have at least four pashminas, three pairs of cashmere socks, one pair of oversized sunglasses (to conceal aforementioned emotional emergency), one stylish hat/headband (to conceal hair-static emergency) and one travel-sized mini-pot of intense moisturizer (to conceal the fact that every last globule of moisture is about to be sucked from your very soul).

Squeeze all of the above into ONE bag and you're a winner!

LEAVING STUFF BEHIND (THE CLOTHING EQUATION)

Depending on where you are emigrating to (and how much space your family/friends have in their wardrobes), it can be handy to leave a few carefully selected 'UK-friendly' clothing items behind.

To explain; if YNC has a fairer climate, why not leave one of your winter coats in Blighty, to save you squeezing it back into your suitcase on every winter visit. Or if your emigration involves leaving the bright lights of a big city and 'going bush', you could always leave a spare pair of heels behind for evenings out on the town with old friends. Essentially, the more luggage-space you have on return trips to the UK, the more shopping goodies you will be able to take back to YNC. Simple wardrobe mathematics!

CHAPTER 15

TWENTY-FOUR HOURS AND COUNTING...

You go Uruguay, and I'll go mine.
GROUCHO MARX[1]

At this stage, there really is no point in writing any more lists. If you haven't thought of it by now, it's too late and not worth worrying about. It's just you and your luggage (and an optional partner – if he hasn't already run for the hills).

It's only natural for Sensible Girls who are hours away from emigrating, to want to spend their last evening with loved ones. If you are emigrating with a partner, this may mean spending it under different roofs, with your respective parents/siblings/friends. But, given that you're only going to have each other's ugly-mugs to look at for the foreseeable foreign future, that shouldn't be an issue.

Some emigrating couples have been known to say their goodbyes on their penultimate evening, getting the emotional stuff out of the way first and then checking into an airport hotel for their last night. The plus side of this strategy is that you can then concentrate on getting yourself together rather than juggling your departure with a highly emotive family farewell. The minus side is that a lot of mums and dads could feel a bit put out if you disappear a day earlier than you really have to.

I would strongly advise that Sensible Single Girls *don't* consider the hotel option and stick with family instead. Spending your last night in a Travelodge, with only a Corby trouser-press and tea-making-facilities for company, could be a tad depressing.

YOUR LAST SUPPER

Whoever you spend your last night with, there are still a few last-minute arrangements to sort out. The centrepiece of this final evening is bound to be dinner...your Last Supper. So if you want to be drinking and eating your favourite things, you need to be a bit creative.

BOOZE

The fact that you didn't have a leaving party on your last night greatly reduces the chances of you being hungover tomorrow morning, but it doesn't completely rule it out. You no doubt still fancy a couple of drinkies this evening, even if it's only to get rid of those pesky butterflies in your stomach. Just go easy on the booze as it's bound to go straight to your head with all this nervous excitement you're experiencing.

If you are staying with guests for your Last Supper, it might be polite if you (plus partner) provide a nice bottle of something for the dinner table. Just remember the Sensible drinking rule: more than a glass, less than a litre.

FOOD

The first question is: will you be dining in or out? There are benefits to both decisions.

If you are heading OUT, choose somewhere tried and tested and maybe stick to local fare as you're not going to get your paws on a decent steak and ale pie for quite some time. Essentially, if you have a favourite type of food, which you won't find easily in YNC, head in that direction.

If you are eating IN we'll presume it will not be in your own house.* A Sensible Girl knows the subtle art of persuasion. Your Last Supper, as with everything else, should be well planned. This can be difficult if it is someone else doing the cooking, as the last thing you want to do is cause offence and appear too pushy. But, you equally don't want to be eating a nice bowl of pasta if you're about to move to Rome. You see my point? To avoid disappointment, have a friendly chat with the Shopper Chef and ask if they would mind awfully if you could choose the *plat du jour*. And it goes without saying to avoid any foodstuffs that may cause flatulence...once airborne, you're likely to puff up like a over inflated balloon – highly unattractive and highly uncomfortable!

Once you have your Last Supper all worked out, there are a couple more packing issues that need to be considered before you're completely done. Try to do this before dinner, rather than after, otherwise you may find yourself uttering that well used phrase. 'Stuff it – I can't be arsed.'

---

* And if this isn't the case, Hello! You're cutting things a little fine aren't you?

LAST-MINUTE LUGGAGE HINTS

- Make sure everything has a lock on it and that you've locked everything. Locking your luggage the night before you leave can help prevent over-emotional parents sneaking in sentimental goodbye cards, teddy bears declaring that you're 'their best friend' or Class A drugs (depending on the type of parents you have).

- Another good reason for locking your luggage early is to avoid a last-minute packing panic. This usually entails the 'victim' (you) running madly around the house, grabbing random objects and thrusting them into your over-full case. Selected items commonly include childhood cuddly toys or family heirlooms. Sensible Girls must remember that a sense of decorum is required at all times – and maybe Mr Bobtail Bunny-wunny-wuffy-kins would prefer to say behind.

- Finally, don't start jumping up and down on your case in despair if you can't squeeze everything in. Remember that there are always courier companies, the Royal Mail

and the prospect of future visiting relatives to help ease
the load. You will also have the opportunity to carry
some more stuff back with you on your next visit.

And when that case is snapped shut and all the locks, clips, tags
and belts are securely fastened...

That's it.

There is nothing left to plan, pack, organise or arrange.

You're done!

CHAPTER 16

AIRPORT DEPARTURE TECHNIQUE

Immigration is the sincerest form of flattery.
JACK PAAR[1]

OK, depending on your exit strategy you will either be leaving the Motherland in a quiet and dignified fashion or in a hysterical, snivelling heap. At this stage, just concentrate on making sure you have everything and everyone in your Leaving Party with you. Sounds simple, but when you've got 101 things on your mind, it's easy to forget something (or someone).

- Passports – 'check'

- Partner – 'check'

- Tickets – 'check'

- Sense of humour – 'Bugger...where did I leave that?'

...you see!

THE AIRPORT LEAVING PARTY
Airport goodbyes can often be a bit rubbish and put a real downer on the trip before you've even started. To avoid a depressing departure, here are a few sensible suggestions to get you on the plane in one piece.

- Now is not the appropriate moment to perfect your 'last on/first off' theory in airport check-in technique. It goes without saying that you must arrive nice and early (especially if there are any luggage issues you need to address). If you are going to be with people who want to give you a nice send-off, make sure there's time for a cuppa before you go 'through'.

- Keep numbers in the party to a minimum – otherwise what started out as a quick cuppa in Deli France could turn into a social event. The more people in the Departure Party, the higher the chance of you being called upon to perform introductions, keep conversations flowing, hand out croissants and generally be the hostess with the mostest. This is the last thing you want at this stage in the proceedings.

- Have some kind of Return Trip Plan. Even if it's a bit of a fib or you might not stick to it, it will be easier for loved ones (and you!) to say au revoir rather than goodbye.

- However tempting it may be to delay goodbyes until the very last minute, this is not recommended. Leave your farewell posse with plenty of time to spare. Aside from the fact that you need at least 45 minutes of quality shopping time in duty free, you also don't want the last words your loved ones hear you cry to be 'Bollocks, they're boarding already', while hurdling the departure gate.

If you are not part of a farewell posse, don't be surprised if you start feeling a bit emotional. Even the most hardened of Sensible Girls feels the odd twinge when leaving the UK as it is a pretty momentous occasion. The most important thing to think about is how much you've achieved to get to this point. And how much more exciting the next part of your journey is going to be.

OK, so this the bit you've been dreading...you're off. Your nose has started running in a very unattractive fashion and you've run out of tissues already. The only thing you have left to wipe it on is a trusty pashmina. Your mum's bottom lip has begun uncontrollably trembling and your dad is studying his shoes in a rather unconvincing manner. It's horrid saying goodbye, so just smile, give everyone a big wet kiss and head for the gate.

It's time for your grand adventure...

You should be incredibly proud of yourself, you've done it!

...or at least the first bit anyway.

Now settle back, relax and enjoy your in-flight emigration entertainment!

A well needed holiday

THE MIDDLE BIT

...IN A LAND FAR, FAR AWAY...

...Three half-watched in-flight movies and numerous inedible airplane meals later, Princess Sally and Lord Grenville arrived in the Western realm of the Great Red Continent – the Kingdom of Perth. They were greeted by Lord Grenville's elder sister, Duchess Lindy of Parkwood, her husband Duke Brian and their son Master Christopher, and whisked away to what would become their home for the next few weeks.

And what a home it was. It had a large watering hole in which one could swim, together with an outdoor cooking fire on which the menfolk roasted meat. There were palm trees in the garden, machines that blew icy air around the house and a large collection of pets, consisting of five canaries, four fish, three cats, two turtle doves and a sheep.

Lord Grenville and the princess liked this Antipodean lifestyle and decided that one day soon they should like to have their very own.

And so began their quest.

First of all they decided to get acclimatised to their new home and spent a week on the beach, doing important research on sun strength, sand texture and all-over-tanning ability. They spent hours leaping through surf and lounging on beach towels and decided that they loved their new country.

Then, amongst all the fun and frivolity, the princess looked up at the clear blue sky and noticed a tiny black cloud hiding behind a palm tree. 'Oh no, what THIS time?' she wondered and tried to have a closer look. It wasn't quite as gloomy as the cloud that followed her around in the UK...but it was annoying nonetheless. After some careful consideration, and a snoop through the local book store's self-help section, she realised it was a Worry Cloud.

While the Worry Cloud bobbed around, following the princess like a fairground balloon, Lord Grenville decided to have a look at rental properties. He selected a couple of salubrious areas in which he felt he and the princess would be happy and began to explore.

But renting one of these properties proved most difficult. Lord Grenville quickly realised that the subjects of Perth had different ways of doing business, unlike anything they had experienced back home. Every time they found a lovely little cottage that they wanted to move into the paperwork went belly-up and they lost it.

The princess began to feel a bit like a young sapling that had been uprooted from the royal court's allotment. It was no good living in someone else's house (however lovely it was). She needed to establish her own roots – and she needed to do this quickly, before she gave up and stormed off home in a huff.

Lord Grenville set forth on his housing hunt and searched the Kingdom of Perth far and wide. He'd viewed 14 castles, one cave and nine hovels that day and was about to give up when he received a call from the Agency of Estates. Apparently an enchanted cottage at the edge of town had become available and would he be interested? It was cheap, needed some superficial work doing and had bags of character.

'Oh dear,' said Lord Grenville. For he was wise in the ways of Agencies of Estates and knew their fancy selling techniques. But with nowhere to live he collected his princess and off they went to look at the property.

It was a huge old ramshackle building surrounded by a jungle of weeds. The front door creaked slowly open and a cockroach the size of a donkey trotted past them into the kitchen. The carpets were a most unusual colour and the bathroom had a suspicious plant growing on the shower curtain. But it had three decent-sized bedrooms, a groovy outdoor entertaining area and was down the road from the pub...so it was perfect. And the princess and Lord Grenville declared that they would move in immediately.

The following morning the princess's cloud had shrunk...just a little.

They loved their enchanted cottage and got to work sprucing things up. With Duke Brian and Duchess Lindy's help, they cleaned and spruced their little house until it shone like a new pin. On the fifth day of scrubbing, Princess Sally stopped, step back and smiled. And her lovely new home smiled back at her.

Now they had somewhere to live. They also had rent to pay, and this meant they needed to find work.

Lord Grenville was delighted to find that the Kingdom of Perth was a rich city built on the wealth of mining and black gold. With all this prosperity knocking around, everyone needed a trusty accountant and so his job hunt began.

The princess was a little less lucky. Even though she'd constantly moaned about her old film publicity job back in London, she now realised that film stars didn't enter the Western Realm of the Red Continent, and she felt a bit anxious. What if she could not find herself another respectable, fabulous sounding, well-paid job? What then?

The cloud grew a bit.

Meanwhile Lord Grenville had been inundated with exciting job offers. The first job he took was in town. The company was BIG. Sadly the boss turned out to be an even bigger idiot. So he left.

The second job he took was out of town. The company was tiny. Everyone was lovely and he enjoyed the work. But the job was just too small. So he left.

The third job he took was halfway in, halfway out of town. It was a permanent position, with lovely people, great perks, decent pay and located ten minutes away from the beach. This job was just right. So he stayed.

Princess Sally was happy for Lord Grenville and relieved that they now had a good income, but her cloud was beginning to annoy her as she felt that it was never going to go away. She might have emigrated elegantly, but she couldn't find a job and she'd not made as single friend either. The princess's bottom lip began to wobble.

So with the cloud in tow, she wandered down to the local shops for some retail therapy. After spending a rather dull five minutes staring at the butcher, the baker and the candlestick maker's window displays, she suddenly noticed a tiny little shop next door. Strange that she hadn't spied it before. It was called The Pink Palace and through the delicate window she saw the most exquisite gowns she had ever laid eyes on. So she gently pushed open the door and went inside.

Everything was fabulous, even the shopkeeper, who had somehow magically appeared next to her as if out of thin air. They got talking. The magical shop keeper turned out to be a good-humoured single mother who was after a new suitor; she needed some time off work because she was treating herself to a brand new Bosom-Job – care of her local plastic surgeon. But she would have to spend a few days in hospital and there was no one to look after her shop. If only she could find someone who was kind, trustworthy, responsible and who had previous experience in retail. OH IF ONLY!

The princess finally understood the true meaning of serendipity and accepted a part-time job as a shop assistant. It might not be the film industry, she told herself, but it's fun, easy and I can work out what I want to do next without joining the Race of the

Rats. And so it came to pass that Lord Grenville and Princess Sally became tax-paying citizens of the Great Red Continent.

And days and weeks ticked by.

And the princess's cloud shrunk until it was barely visible...but you could still just see it, if you squinted.

At the black gold factory Lord Grenville was busy making friends. A flagon of ale with his colleagues or a round of golf with the boss – he was truly settling into his new job. Unfortunately for the princess, there were no other employees to befriend aside from the magical shopkeeper (who now proudly supported a cleavage the size of Cheddar Gorge). So she decided to be proactive in such matters for if friends were not going to find the princess...she would have to go out and find them!

The princess enrolled on a course to become a swimming instructor. The kids were nice, but the staff were horrid, so she left.

The princess joined an art class and leant how to draw apples on tablecloths. The people were nice, but she didn't really have anything in common with any of them.

The princess took her box full of empty wine and beer bottles out to her recycling bin on a Sunday morning and bumped into a girl carrying a similar load.

'Ummm...it's taken us a month to get through this lot,' lied the princess.

'That's nothing, it's taken two days to get through this,' said her neighbour 'Gidday, I'm Mrs Galah. Fancy a cuppa?'

And so the friendship began.

Mr and Mrs Galah lived in the cottage opposite and, never having met their neighbours, had resigned themselves to the fact that they were probably quiet, retiring teetotallers. However, later that evening, upon dropping round to Princess Sally and Lord Grenville's enchanted (and fully renovated) cottage for a couple of drinks, they changed their minds and opened another bottle of Shiraz!

Amongst the drunken haze that evening, the princess looked up and noticed that for the first time since she'd arrived in the Great Red Continent her little black cloud had completely vanished.

It was also around this time that the princess decided to start writing. Emigrating had been a life-changing experience for her and one that was still evolving. She felt strongly that there were so many people back in Londinium and beyond that would be so much happier if they escaped the city and moved to where the sun shone and the dolphins squeaked, so she made it her duty to enlighten them.

So she wrote...

And she wrote...

And she wrote...

In the meantime Princess Sally's beloved parents, King John and Queen Carolyn, came to visit. They had not been impressed by their daughter's decision to emigrate to a cultureless wasteland in the Back of Beyond, and thought they might be able to change her mind.

She changed their minds.

And they went home and made enquiries about retirement visas.

And so she continued to write.

And she wrote...

And she wrote...

And when she finished writing she sent her book to anyone she thought might be interested, for she knew not of the mystical ways of the book publisher.

Beloved friends came to visit. They were bemused by this strange life that Lord Grenville and the princess had carved out for themselves and wanted to view it for themselves (as one would view a strange two-headed goblin or a giant beanstalk).

They liked what they saw. It made sense. So they went home and made enquiries about skilled visas.

A whole year had passed since they first landed in the Great Red Continent.

Princess Sally awoke one morning with a hangover. She and Lord Grenville had spent the evening with their neighbours, drinking ale and cooking various pieces of meat on their outdoor fire. It had been fun. She stumbled out to the mail box and flicked through the junk mail.

'Reader's Indigestion – you have won 5000 pieces of gold'

'Collect your free goat when you buy five hoggets'

'The Three Little Pigs Housing Fund – please give generously'

The final envelope was from a publishing company called A & C Black of Londinium and had a wax seal on it.

Princess Sally opened the envelope with trembling hands...

...and fainted.

~~THE END~~

TO BE CONTINUED...

THE SENSIBLE GIRL'S IN-FLIGHT QUIZ

(Well, it's not like you've got anything else to do)

QUESTION ONE
How would you describe your emigrating experience so far?

A)   A beautiful, joyous journey of self discovery.
B)   A bloody miracle.
C)   A stressful, testing and rewarding step towards finding a better life abroad.

QUESTION TWO
Why is it a sensible idea to leave the UK and live somewhere else?

A)   Because the UK population has reached 60 million and there are no parking spaces left.
B)   Because in a recent survey, 92 per cent of Brits found that they were 'happier living abroad than they were in the UK'.[1]
C)   Because the whispering voices inside my head told me to.

QUESTION THREE
How many alcoholic drinks have you had since take off?

A)   None.
B)   One or more.
C)   ...Umm, should I include the bottle of champers I had in the departure lounge?

QUESTION FOUR
For those who chose to sell their house – how would you rate your removal men?

A)   I'd have been better off inviting Mr Blobby to come and pack my valuables.
B)   Satisfactory, although I could have done without the arse cleavage.
C)   Ask me when I unpack everything at the other end.

QUESTION FIVE
For those who chose to rent out their house – how would you rate your new tenants?

A)   I'm pleased I'm not living next door to them.
B)   I'm pleased I'm not living in the same country as them.
C)   I'll be checking for any fresh excavations under the patio when we next return.
D)   I'm very happy with them...and our neighbours are even happier now that WE'VE gone!

QUESTION SIX
Did you get an upgrade?

A)   Yes.
B)   No.

QUESTION SEVEN
What culinary delights do you have on your in-flight meal tray?

A)   A cold, mushy starter involving unidentifiable tinned fish, grated carrot and a grape.
B)   A hot beef or chicken main dish (not the one you wanted because they'd run out) served with diced potatoes or rice, more carrots and some suspicious-looking gravy.
C)   A pink, square, gelatinous, mousse-like dessert with a squirty cream garnish.
D)   A very solid bread roll and vacuum packed sweaty faux-cheddar cheese.
E)   A hair.
F)   Nothing yet – I'm still perusing the menu while nibbling on a canapé.

QUESTION EIGHT
What do you expect to achieve within the first month of arriving in YNC?

A)   An all-over tan, natural highlights and a greater understanding of the celebrity wedding phenomenon – thanks to *OK* magazine.

B) To have a job interview lined up and a good idea of where I want to live, to know where the best shoe shops are, and to develop a greater understanding of my new country's public transport system.

C) To avoid having a nervous breakdown and jumping on the first flight home.

QUESTION NINE

Who will be meeting you at the airport?

A) Mr Nobody...sniff!

B) My aunt/uncle/brother/sister/cousin/best friend/ relocation manager.

C) My boss's wife's hairdresser/my hairdresser's wife's boss/my wife's boss's hairdresser.

QUESTION TEN

What scares you most about emigrating?

A) The Future.

B) Leaving loved ones behind.

C) How I'll cope without chocolate Hob Nobs.

QUESTION ELEVEN

What do you want to learn most about your new fellow countrymen?

A) Everything – their culture/religion/customs/ history/drinking habits/inside leg measurement.

B) Nothing – who cares, they're just a bunch of foreigners.

QUESTION TWELVE

What were the main reasons for your emigration?

A)   To find a more relaxed and fulfilling lifestyle in
     sunnier climes.
B)   To jump bail and give the cops the slip.
C)   To seek out exciting business opportunities and
     improve my career.
D)   To prove to my unsupportive Ex-Reluctant-Partner
     just how fabulous and daring I really am!

QUESTION FOURTEEN

Back in the UK, who do you think is going to miss you
the most?

A)   My mum and dad.
B)   My best friend.
C)   My ex-boyfriend.
D)   My boyfriend.
E)   My landlord at the local pub.

QUESTION FIFTEEN

If you had to go through the whole emigrating process
again, what would you do differently?

A)   I'd try to not get so stressed about the smaller
     details. If some silly mare at the Vintage Clothing
     Store doesn't want to pay more than twenty quid
     for my Diane Von Furstenburg dress, that's her
     problem.

B)   I'd learn to delegate and make use of emigration agents, relocation companies, accountants, quarantine specialists, psychiatrists, friends and relations.

C)   My hair.

QUESTION SIXTEEN
What's the most useless thing you've emigrated with?

A)   My boyfriend.

B)   My 23-year-old arthritic cat.

C)   My mum's hand me down Mini Metro.

D)   My negative attitude.

E)   There is nothing useless about my emigration, thank you!

QUESTION SEVENTEEN
If there had been a soundtrack to your UK departure, what would it have been?

A)   She's Leaving Home – The Beatles.

B)   We've Gotta Get Out of this Place – The Animals.

C)   I Will Survive – by Gloria Gaynor.

D)   Breathe – The Prodigy.

E)   The Funeral March – Chopin.

F)   So Long, Farewell – The Sound of Music.

QUESTION EIGHTEEN
Have you stopped crying since you said your goodbyes?

A)   Yes.
B)   No.
C)   Pah! I never started.

QUESTION NINETEEN
Where do you hope to 'be' this time next year?

A)   Living in a nice house with my partner, working in a job that I enjoy, having made some new friends.
B)   Living in a beach-side castle, with a fabulous job, a statue in my honour and a shed load of servants.
C)   On the 207 heading towards Shepherds Bush.
D)   I have no idea, I can't even imagine where I'll be next week.

QUESTION TWENTY
If you were to get stopped at customs in YNC – what might they find hidden in your suitcase?

A)   Half a pound of Lincolnshire sausages.
B)   Half a pound of Granny Smiths.
C)   Three kilos of Smarties.
D)   A can of baked beans.
E)   The entire contents of a Fortnum and Mason's hamper.

SCORES:

QUESTION ONE	QUESTION TWO	QUESTION THREE
A) -10 freak	A) 10	A) 0
B) 10	B) 10	B) 10
C) 10	C) -10	C) 20

QUESTION FOUR	QUESTION FIVE	QUESTION SIX
A) -10	A) to C) -10	A) 1000
B) 10	D) 20	B) 0
C) 20		

QUESTION SEVEN	QUESTION EIGHT	QUESTION NINE
A) to D) 10	A) 10	A) 100 brave girl
E) -20	B) 20	B) 10 Sensible Girl
F) 100	C) 10	C) 20 resourceful girl

QUESTION TEN	QUESTION ELEVEN	QUESTION TWELVE
A) + B) 10 – you'll be fine	A) 10	A) 10
	B) -50 not quite the attitude we're after	B) -100...OK
D) -10 – you'll lose weight		C) 10
		D) 20 show off!

QUESTION FOURTEEN*
(* there's no 13)

A) 10
B) 10
C) -50 who cares?
D) -10 why isn't he sitting next to you?
E) 0 two words... Betty Ford

QUESTION FIFTEEN

A) 10
B) 20
C) 0

QUESTION SIXTEEN

A) 0 that's not nice
B) 0
C) 0
D) 0
E) 100

QUESTION SEVENTEEN

A) to F) 10

QUESTION EIGHTEEN

A) 10
B) 10
C) 0 you hard girl

QUESTION NINETEEN

A) 10
B) -50 hello - reality check!
C) 0
D) 10

QUESTION TWENTY

A) + B) -50 release the sniffer dogs!
C) + D) 10 very sensible
E) 100...that's my girl!

WELL...

What are you waiting for? Start totting up your score!

RESULTS:

-380 TO 0	**SILLY GIRL** Dig out the imaginary dunce hat, find a corner of the plane (admittedly that's a tricky one!), and go and sit in it as soon as the seatbelt signs are switched off. Then consider re-doing this quiz when you've calmed down! Good grief! You need to pull your in-flight-socks up, lady! You CAN do this you know... you just need to really want to!
0 TO 120	**SENSIBLE GIRL** Push the 'Attendant' button and order yourself another glass of wine. You deserve it. You've got a sensible and realistic attitude to what YNC has to offer and you are both excited and nervous about settling in. Don't worry, with such an open outlook you're bound to make a go of it!

120 TO INFINITY

SUPER GIRL

Is it a bird...is it a plane...no, it's a rather glamorous British gal who's about to take her new country by storm.

Dharlink – your emigration is truly elegant, but just make sure your expectations are not *too* high, otherwise you might be heading for a fall.

Take a leaf out of the Sensible Girl's book and keep those feet firmly planted on the ground... well, when you land anyway!

CHAPTER 17

AIRPORT ARRIVAL TECHNIQUE

Depending on the locality of your emigration destination (and whether you were able to take a holiday en route), you will now look like one of the following when exiting the plane:

A particularly static flight	A limited legroom flight
A totally sleepless flight	A rather boozy flight

It's all about first impressions and none of these is quite what you're after. If you are being met by some kind soul who is helping you settle in to YNC, you want to avoid scaring them. So why not pop into the airport loo for a couple of minutes and at least comb your hair, wipe away your red wine moustache and brush those peanut crumbs and dried snot off your pashmina.

That's much better...

Keep pushing that trolley through the airport towards the exit sign. You've left your old life behind and you're about to enter into your brand new one. This is the beginning of your adventure. Your New Life officially starts right here, right now.

All you need to think about for the moment is getting yourself from the airport to your accommodation. If you're fortunate enough have a friend, relative or relocation agent meeting and greeting you, relax, kick back and familiarise yourself with your new surroundings. If you're on your tod, check in to where you will be staying for the next few days/weeks/months – and do exactly the same thing!

To enjoy your emigration, you need to enjoy yourself! So go with the flow. No over-analysing everyone as you push your luggage through the airport. No snap decisions as to whether this emigrating malarkey was a huge mistake, while you're getting into the taxi. Just observe without judgement. Think of yourself as a giant, but rather attractive, sponge! You just want to absorb everything and leave all of your prejudice, pre-judgements and negativity with Lost Luggage.

Another way of looking at your brand new future is to see YNC as a fabulous new boyfriend. Expat coaches Sabina and Nynke like to compare emigrating to starting a new relationship when coaching newly arrived boys and girls about settling into their new life abroad:[1]

'During the exciting time of being "in love", everything looks great. You've got that holiday feeling. But when you get married [emigrate], the reality of everyday life kicks in. Then it is important to realise that in a good marriage, you have to make YOURSELF happy and rather than expecting your partner [that's YNC] to do it for you. Enjoy the company of your partner [YNC] instead of expecting too much from him.'

So come on...feel the love! After all, it's the beginning of your fabulous new foreign future!

CHAPTER 18

SETTLING IN

Woo Hoo!
HOMER SIMPSON

NOW we're getting down to the nitty-gritty.

You have officially emigrated. Give the girl a gold star! But having planned every last minutiae of your emigration for what seems like an eternity, suddenly you've actually got to get out there and 'do stuff'. Your New Country is no longer an abstract place that you dreamt about, it has just become Your New Home (YNH) and how you settle in will affect exactly how homely it feels. So, without further ado, we need to embark on the final stage of your Master Plan. We need to gather all of your emigration tools and start spinning a few foreign plates.

SETTLING-IN CHECKLIST

As we've already established, no single book, website or person is going to have the magical solution to all of your emigration enigmas, so the more resourceful you are the better. It's time to dig out those emigration tools and get busy.

- Country-specific emigrating book
- Country-specific travel guidebook
- Bilingual dictionary/phrase book

- Emigration websites
  - UK-based, giving British expats practical advice on how to settle down, i.e. specific to WHO you are and WHERE you've emigrated from. Particularly good for any final loose-end-tying.
- Immigration websites
  - YNH-based, advising how immigrants from all nations settle in, i.e. specific to where you NOW are and WHAT'S on offer out there. Particularly good for further Seed Planting.
- Expat websites
  - Offering a plethora of advice, these websites usually have chat rooms as well, where you can meet fellow Sensible Boys and Girls in YNH and either find out where to buy a Double Decker...or discover what social events are on offer.
- Immigration agencies
- Relocation agencies
- Official/governmental websites
  Depending on the quality of the site, these can offer advice on the bureaucracy you'll be up against once you settle down assist you in finding out about health, welfare, job schemes, tax, etc.
- Emigration literature
  You can sign up for emigration newsletters or subscribe to an emigration magazine. Both of which will give you up-to-date information.
- Job, bank and property websites
- Newspapers (national/local)

When it comes to emigrating elegantly, the Internet becomes a Sensible Girl's best friend. So, as usual, you will find yourself notching up a lot of online hours. I would just like to make one small (rather motherly) comment about this because, while online research is really important, leaving the house and getting 'out there' is too. This is the final stage of your emigration so it's no good permanently planting yourself in front of your PC, starving yourself of natural light and turning into a little mushroom. The most important thing for you to do is interact with YNH in person, you've got to get out there and explore!

Because you did so dazzlingly well with your Seed Planting back in the UK, you are already en route to settling down in YNH.

And as you know, goal setting is the best way to focus your efforts on successfully achieving everything you want. You're looking for a great job and fabulous new home, some new friends or even a boyfriend. But amidst these key factors that you are manically scribbling down (don't forget the convertible and the swimming pool, oh...and the walk-in wardrobe) are some less obvious goals that will make you stop and think to yourself, 'Wow, this really *is* my new home.' It could be when you move in to your first rental property, or when your container of belongings arrive. It could be when you get invited out by your work colleagues for the first time or when you manage your first conversation in YNH's mother tongue.

All of these goals and objectives blend together to form Your New Life, and while I've tried to pick out a few key topics to get you started, your list will be ongoing and infinite. You see, once you get going, it's like writing a letter to Santa. There are just so many things a Sensible Girl wants when she's settling into her new country. Today it's a rental property but a year later it may be upgraded to buying a house. Likewise, you might currently be admiring your recently acquired temporary visa, but five years from now, maybe citizenship will be your newly chosen goal.

Essentially, the following list really only includes the basics. The longer you live in YNH, the bigger and more complicated your list becomes (and the less it has to do with emigration!).

PAPERWORK

Now that you have legally entered YNH, is there anything else you need stamping, signing, approving, registering or renewing? Is there any other documentation you need to apply for? Is your quest for a more permanent residency ongoing? Do you have more bureaucracy to fight your way through, now that you're here? Depending on where YNH is, there could be extra paperwork to sign off on before you can relax. Don't slack off now: keep on top of your foreign paperwork, get yourself a new box file and keep plugging away.

Do you need to apply for a new driver's licence, tax file number, bank account (see next section), dental registration, medical card or golf club membership? Dig out all of those beautiful passport photographs you had done before leaving and get to work.

Have you registered with the British Consulate? This will help them keep in touch with you if there are any problems in your country.

Have you made sure you can still vote back in the UK? Because so long as you were registered before you left, you can still take part in general elections.

FINANCE

If you have not already opened a bank account, pull your finger out and do it now.* But familiarise yourself with the banks and account options in YNH as they may have different systems (and bank charges!) than they did back in Blighty.

Keep an eye on your UK accounts via the Internet. If you have travelled to YNH via a couple of holiday-stopovers, it's always wise to keep a check on potential card-cloning situations. Likewise, if you are expecting regular deposits in to your bank account care of your newly ensconced tenants back in Britain, make sure payments are received.

Save a 'cash converter' (which will automatically have its exchange rate updated) into your Favourites on your computer,

---

* Or as soon as you have a permanent address (and any other necessary requirements).

as this will help you keep an eye on the financial markets and decide when it is the right time to bring your sterling over. If you plan on using a financial broker to oversee this transfer, select a reputable company and start a dialogue with someone so you can feel more comfortable about giving the green light when the time is right.

Try to keep your transfers from UK accounts to a minimum as, depending on the terms of your account, you will be charged for each transaction. This means making larger/fewer ATM withdrawals than you probably did back home (i.e. €250 each withdrawal, as opposed to '10 quid a day depending on whether you needed fags or not').

RENTING

Unless you already have super-strong ties to YNH or you are completely minted, we'll presume that you'll be looking at renting a property before buying.

The first thing you will need to do is some mental arithmetic so that you can work out a rental budget based on YNH's salary. If you haven't found yourself a job yet, estimate what you hope to bring home each month (see next section on Employment for tips) and go from there. Ask questions about properties you're interested in, to get a rough idea of what bills and other costs you will bet hit with. Also consider any other expenditure that you are likely to encounter over the next few months while settling down. For example, have you bought a car yet or finished paying for storage and shipping? Add and subtract everything, allow a bit of leeway for error (remember your cash cushion!) and stick to the final figure you come up with.

You might encounter a 'chicken and egg' scenario when you first try to locate a rental agency or landlord willing to lease to you – i.e. you can't find a job until you've got somewhere to live, but you can't find somewhere to live until you've got a job to pay for it. You should be able to convince these people of your 'model tenant' status, by offering a peek at any substantial savings accounts you have, together with any character references you can supply them with. If you still find that you are having problems, relocation companies in your area might be able to recommend tried and tested agencies that are used to dealing with new arrivals with no 'financial history'. So have a chat to them and see what they suggest.

Once you feel that your finances are in order (or at least lined up and ready to go), you can move on to the fun bit. Finding your first rental property.

The chances are you will not be as familiar with YNH as you were back in GB, so do your research and get a good idea of the areas you like and whether you can afford them. To avoid confusion keep your search area limited to a handful of places so that you can really concentrate on familiarising yourself with them (two or three should keep you nice and focused).

Aside from choosing locations that are practical and affordable, try to find something that is going to make you *happy*. After all, settling down in YNH was meant to be an improvement on life back in the UK and in the first few formative months of your emigration, being happy in your new home will help you establish roots. On the other hand, any rash decisions you make moving into properties that are wrong for you, could simply make you throw all of your toys out of the proverbial pram and want to go 'home'.

To avoid post-emigration strops and help you find a sensible rental property, ask yourself a few of the following questions.

- **Do you have specific location requirements?** Do you have kids (school), a dog (nearby park), are you an exercise freak (gym) or do you want to surf every morning (beach)?
- **Will you feel safe in the areas you've chosen?** Moving into a neighbourhood that turns out to be Gangsta Alley – requiring a bulletproof vest to be worn whenever you pop out for a pint of milk – is to be avoided. So try to find out what these places are like after dark, if only to check out the surrounding nightlife, see how the locals are and whether you'd be happy getting around on your own – stuff you took for granted back home, but you can't be 100 per cent sure about over here. Just because it's busy and groovy during the day, it doesn't mean to say things are going to be so rosy once the sun goes down. You need to do a stake-out.
- **What type of home are you after?** The areas you choose will probably determine this – if you're looking for something central, for example, you will probably have to go for the apartment option. If, on the other hand, you are moving

somewhere a bit more rural, opt for the three-bedroom cottage.

- **Do you want a furnished or unfurnished property?** This will depend on when you plan to ship your storage container over (if you haven't done so already). You could be testing the water and keeping everything in the UK until further notice, in which case you need fully furnished. Or your stuff might be about to rock up on a boat, in which case you will need to make do with an unfurnished pad while you are waiting for it to arrive.

- **How many bedrooms are you after?** It's a good idea to try to get somewhere with more than one, if only to up the chances of you receiving UK visitors. Kipping on the sofa for two weeks is probably not going to appeal to everyone who's toying with the idea of visiting you – especially not your mum and dad!

- **Do you need a parking space** or do you just need somewhere to chain your bike? Are you near public transport? If so, what is the commute like (see Getting Around, page 248)?

The final thing you need to consider when renting your first property in YNH is what length lease to sign. Back in the UK, this might not have been such an issue, but over here things seem a bit more complicated as you're not really sure what you'll be up to next weekend, let alone in six months' time.

Many people who emigrate understandably try to avoid any type of property commitment until they have a much clearer plan of what they want to do next. So they sign a six-month lease. This is a great way of keeping options open and allows people the freedom to make further adjustments to their emigration plans if things don't quite work out. It also allows Sensible Girls the option of getting back on the property ladder, after six short months, to purchase their very own place in the sun.

Just be aware that when you sign a six-month lease, you are still very new to YNH. You will need to swot up on new areas and start viewing potential new properties pretty soon after you move in. Bearing in mind that you are still familiarising yourself with the local neighbourhood and possibly don't even have your furniture yet (let alone a stable job and three months' worth of payslips to enable you to apply for a mortgage), you could find yourself needing a little more time. And aside from the fact that landlords generally like their tenants to sign longer leases (thus securing them a longer guaranteed income), it would be a complete pain to get booted out after six months and have to find another rental before you're ready to buy.

The flip-side of this equation is that you sign a contract that ties you in for, say two years. If, a few months later you decide you do want to make a few changes (maybe buy a house or rent in another area), things can get fiddly and you'll need to think about breaking from your contract, which may be expensive.

Yes...it's yet another emigration conundrum and as ever, there is no single gold-plated answer. You need to work through the options and puzzle it out for yourself. And when you do work it out and decide where you want to rent and how long you want to rent for, be completely clear about the type of contract you will be required to sign. The 'pretend' one you may have had back in the UK when renting off a mate will be nothing compared to this, plus YNH could have different terms and conditions to what you are used to. The last thing you want to do is tie yourself into something you're not 101 per cent happy with, or indeed clear about. So if you don't understand something, or the paperwork is not written in English and you're not absolutely fluent in YNH's language *don't sign anything* until you get a bit of help or translation.

EMPLOYMENT

Even though you might feel as if you're on a lovely, long holiday, you're not. And sooner or later you're going to have to get a job. If you've been sensible (and lucky) enough to stash a bit of cash before the 'big move', you may have a few free weeks to get yourself organised, but try not to put things off too long as you may find yourself losing your nerve. Starting a new job in the UK is daunting enough, but starting something in a foreign country? With foreigners? Possibly speaking a foreign language? Scary!

A good place to start your search is with some nice, friendly recruitment agencies. Hopefully you've already spoken to these chaps on either your recce visits or via e-mail, so now it's time to put them to work.

First of all your CV will probably need upgrading so that it is appropriate to the job market in which you will now be searching. A helpful agency should have a look at your UK CV and give you a few pointers.

SENSIBLE CV UPGRADE

- Have you amended your new contact details?
- Have you updated work dates since leaving the UK?
- Does it need translating?
- Does all the terminology you've used make sense to local employers or is it too anglicised?
- Is it too long (or too short) for YNC's requirements?
- Are you looking for a different position to the one you had in the UK. In which case, have you down-played irrelevant experience and bigged-up relevant skills?
- In fact, it's a good idea to tailor your CV to each type of job you apply for. Save different copies (i.e. one for Marketing, one for General Office Work, one for Retail etc...)
- Have you included e-mail and website addresses of past employers/companies, so anyone interested in you can do a quick spot of research? Just because we are all familiar with UK based companies, employers in YNC might not be, which can make your CV harder to decipher.
- Is it worthwhile attaching copies of your pre-written references?

Find out whether there are any different interview or application techniques in place in YNH that you should be aware of? Ask your recruitment agent as many questions as you need to, so that you are well prepared.

It's good to know what the job market is like generally, as well as in your particular line of work, but most importantly you need to start ascertaining exactly what you are worth. While converting future pay cheques back into sterling is always interesting, we all know that it's now irrelevant. Be prepared for a disparity with past wages, but don't start celebrating or commiserating about this variation just yet, as it's all relative. So long as you're being offered the going rate in YNH and the fact you can afford to rent 'that divine condo with river glimpses'...is all that matters right now. Remember to cast your net wide, as the more agencies you visit, the better idea you'll get of what you're worth.

Keep a close watch on the job sections of local/national newspapers (and Internet sites) and don't be afraid to go for jobs in which you're not totally interested. The interview experience will come in handy and prepare you for the Dream Job you're really after – especially if you're practising your new language.

And while we're on the subject of dream jobs, please do yourself a favour when you're looking through YNC's job vacancies and be open-minded. Ticking all the right boxes in one fell swoop is admirable but unlikely when you've only just arrived in YNC. And so while you obviously deserve 'the best' in all aspects of your emigration, you need to know when a bit of compromise is in order. There is nothing wrong with taking a job that isn't what you did back in the UK and, although it's not ideal, there is nothing wrong with taking a wage drop either – as long as you can absorb the financial hit and some of your 'boxes' get ticked as a result. YNC's career path is just that – a path – and it doesn't stop at the first job you get. You may need to go through a few jobs before you hit the jackpot, so view this as a work in progress.

Lastly, if you are starting up your own business, try to talk to other people who are in the same line of work (while being sensitive that you're about to become their competition), research new business schemes that are available and see if there are any government financial incentives knocking around that could assist in the set-up costs. And if all else fails, search out your new bank manager...and send him or her a very big bunch of flowers!

STARTING A NEW JOB OVERSEAS

Of course, employment challenges don't just stop when you start a foreign job. Nope, they just come at you from a slightly different direction. You will be the New Girl in more ways than one (which is not always a bad thing – read on!), so make a mental note of the following tips before your first day in the office.

BE AWARE OF 'FOREIGN OFFICE POLITICS'

Photocopying your boobs and surprising a workmate at your Christmas party might have been a laugh back at your old job, but it's always a good idea to watch and learn before signing up to be the new office prankster. Work ethics and office etiquette could be a little different in YNH so be sure of how things work. Punctuality, leaving times, coffee breaks, work output, office pecking-orders, you name it; they might all be a tad different from what you're used to so ask your boss first and then your new workmates, so you get a balanced picture of what is required from you (and what isn't!).

START AS YOU MEAN TO GO ON

We all like to make a good first impression, but if you emigrated for a lifestyle upgrade, don't get sucked in to making your office YNH. Get the job done, but give yourself a sensible time limit and if you've not finished by then, *go home*. Easier said than done, but if you always work late or arrive early, it will start to be anticipated rather than appreciated and you didn't leave GB to stare at a computer all day! It might feel awkward at first, but you need to get the balance right otherwise you'll just replicate your stressy UK lifestyle, rather than start a relaxing new one.

YOU'RE NEWER THAN NEW!

Most people start a new job feeling...well...new. They don't know where the kettle is or where the loos are. You, on the other hand, may have the added challenge of not knowing where your office is, where the street where your office is, or even where the town where the street is...where your office is. You won't know what TV show everyone is talking about when you venture into the kitchen to find the kettle. And you certainly won't know all the in jokes that you used to take for granted back with your British workplace buddies. Essentially, it feels like you don't actually know anything!

But don't worry. Nice people (the ones you *want* to make friends with) are always happy to help. They can explain what bus route you should be taking, where to get your lunch, or what's good on telly. You're a novelty, you're shiny and new. Milk it! (see Chapter 21).

Sensible Single Girls should especially take note (and advantage) of this virginal status, as you will be able to play the Scared Little Bunny card when meeting the Dish of the office. Which may be very non-PC...but is also very effective when bagging yourself a boyfriend.

IT'S NOTHING PERSONAL

So you've been in your new job for exactly one month and *no one* has asked you to join them for a drink. It's not like they all go out together and ignore you, but you've not had one single social invitation.

Relax, it's nothing personal. First of all, depending on YNC's culture, maybe your work colleagues are a bit more reserved than back in Blighty. Or maybe they have family commitments and don't have time. Imagine if a 'Jenny Foreigner' arrived when you were working at your old job. Would you have dropped everything and asked them to join you and all of your mates – probably not! Seek solace in the fact that British girls are one of the more cliquey breeds of female to walk the planet, especially when they're en masse on home turf. Luckily for you, other countries can be a bit more welcoming, so be patient in your quest for a 'bezzie' and in the meantime make a few hints about going for a glass of wine after work.

IF YOU DON'T KNOW SOMETHING...ASK!
Self explanatory, simple – don't be shy!

SOCIAL LIFE
Or maybe I should say lack of it. Because, there's a strong chance that your diary might look a little bit tragic at the moment. Try not to worry; it's only natural for a Sensible Girl to feel socially stunted upon arrival in her new country.

As I've already mentioned, there are plenty of emigration tools that will assist in the friend-finding process. So rather than bang on about these, here are a few 'getting out into the fresh air' options for you to try as well (please note that Sensible Single girls can use some of the following techniques to meet prospective boyfriends too!).

FINDING A 'LOCAL'
Very important.

Whether it's a coffee shop, noodle bar or late night diner, it's good to have a couple of regular haunts where you (and your partner) can hang out. This won't necessarily assist in finding friends, but it will help you to absorb yourself in YNH's society and make you feel like you're part of it. One of the key issues of settling in to YNH is feeling like you belong and a smiley barista who knows how you take your coffee every morning is a definite start.

WORKMATES

OK, so we've established that this can take time, but one of the easiest ways to settle in to YNH and make some friends is through your new job. It's a kind of forced integration, which, depending on your workplace and work colleagues, could be just what your social calendar needed. For the first couple of months, try to say 'yes' to as many work/social invitations as you can possibly manage, just to get yourself out there and meet as many potential buddies as possible. Then, once you've worked out who you want to play with (and who you don't), you can calm down a bit and stay in on 'school nights' – if you want to of course!

FELLOW FOREIGNER

You *love* YNH, but when you've had a bad day and everything (and everyone) is pissing you off, there's nothing better than a good old-fashioned whinge. But recently emigrated Sensible Girls can feel a bit self-conscious about slagging off their new country (or its inhabitants) to someone who was born and bred there. What you need is a like-minded expat who understands where you're coming from.

After a bit of Googling, you should be able to track down a nice group of supportive expats to assist in your mission to settle in. You may find British associations, chat rooms, dating websites, sporting clubs, social events – you name it – and it's likely that your local expatriate community has thought of it.

But you're not just confined to the computer when meeting new people. In fact, it has been known to make friends without relying on the Internet, and actually meet someone in the flesh! Spotting expats can become a bit of a game – rather like I Spy. For example, it's a lot easier to spot one in a foreign-speaking country (for obvious reasons). Rosanne Knorr, author of *The Grown-Up's Guide to Running Away from Home*, observes:[1]

'If a person spoke English but didn't carry a camera, it was a clue they weren't the average tourist.'

Likewise, clothing can be a dead give-away and us Brits are often easy to spot. For example, British blokes usually wear T-shirts whereas Aussie blokes often wear vests. 'Yes', you can stereotype with these observations...but who cares, it's good fun!

Whatever your method, if you start with a bit of friendly chit-chat, you could be surprised where it may lead. I know people who have made friends in supermarkets, doctor's surgeries children's playgrounds and so on. In fact, the potential is anywhere where people are standing still long enough to start small talk. And once that small talk starts, you get the opportunity to get a few things off your chest – and that can be a huge relief!

DO IT FOR CHARITY

If you can't bring yourself to go up to complete strangers and ask them to be your friend, why not do it in the name of charity instead? YNH is bound to have a few charity organisations that are crying out for an extra pair of hands and with a half-empty social diary, you've got plenty of time to donate. Try to get creative with your choice of organisation, as this can not only open friendship doors, but also give rise to opportunities to enjoy brand new experiences.

DO SOMETHING FABULOUS

It's a known (although unscientific) fact that people are drawn to other fabulous people. So if you're hobbies are needlepoint and Suduko, try to come up with something a little bit more exotic to get people interested. Be daring. Learn an extreme sport or take up pole dancing. Try a drama class or learn to belly-dance. Aside from making friends with the people who will be attending the same classes as you, you will also have something impressive to say when your new work colleagues ask, 'So what did you get up to at the weekend?'

SPORT

This category can be divided in two; girls who want to play and girls who want to watch – and both are great ways to meet people.

If you're keen to play, pick a sport and get fit at the same time as making friends. If you would prefer to sit on the sidelines and spectate, select a sport that you fancy getting a bit fanatical about and pick a team (preferably a local one). Buy a piece of kit identifying that you support 'said team'. Go to a game and have a ball...and some common ground when you go to your local afterwards!

KIDS

If you are a Sensible Mum who's having trouble finding friends, use the kids! There could well be mother and baby groups, clinics, coffee mornings and the like, similar to the ones that you had access to back in the UK. Even sitting in the local playground with your little ones could get you talking to a like-minded Mum. The trick is to try to get out there as much as possible. If you're not sure where to head, ask your new GP to point you in the right direction or look in the local press.

TOURISTS

You might well be a permanent resident of YNH, but that doesn't mean to say you can't do a bit of sightseeing, especially if you're still a bit hazy about where everything is. Pretending to be a tourist is a great way of finding your way around town and enjoying yourself. And if you're feeling a bit lonely, you'll probably get to chat to some friendly foreigners (maybe even a few Brits on holiday) in the process.

PETS

Our pooches aren't picky. They like smelling doggie bottoms whether they belong to an English, French or American dog, so take your four-legged friend for his morning walk and get chatting to other pet owners. It's a start – not a very glamorous one...but it's a start!

BACK IN BLIGHTY

Be aware that starting out in a new country can make you a teeny bit more vulnerable. It's nothing to worry about; you just need to remember that back in the UK someone usually knew where you were and what you were up to, whereas in YNH this may not always be the case, especially if you're Sensible and Single. This is purely because you don't know that many people yet and obviously this will change with time. But, for the moment, try to stay in regular communication with your friends and family back home. Let them know what you're up to and where you're doing it. Aside from helping with your homesickness, they'll be reassured by keeping tabs on you for the first few weeks.

Don't forget about your friends back in the UK either, as they're going to want to hear all the goss about how you're getting on. There are loads of communication options out there so the fact that your best friend now lives over the Atlantic, rather than over the road, should not stop you having a decent natter now and then.

Utilise the services of Facebook, MySpace or the like and upload some photos of you and YNC. There's something very satisfying about receiving positive feedback and compliments about 'how lovely everything looks' from your friends in the UK, which quietly affirms your decision to emigrate and makes you feel lucky and happy to be there. Show off a little, too: after all, all these positive vibes will prove very helpful when warding off an attack of homesickness.

Finally, make sure all of your UK-based family and friends have *your* new contact details so that they can fill you in on all of their gossip (life does carry on without you, I'm afraid). Make sure everyone has a phone number for you and don't forget to give people the full phone number as grannies can sometimes get confused by country codes. Likewise, when you move into your new home, remember to give everyone the address as it's always nice to get something in the post (especially when it's coming up to Christmas or your birthday). Skype addresses, new e-mail addresses, new mobile numbers...dish them out ASAP, so you don't feel cut off from your old life.

GETTING AROUND
If you are moving to a town or city, get yourself the equivalent of an *A–Z*.

If you feel like having a stab at YNH's public transport system, arm yourself with timetables and don't try to conquer the entire bus or train network in one afternoon. Concentrate on the areas where you think you'd like to live and become familiar with a few key routes. If you're planning on commuting to work using public transport, find out how long it takes from where you want to live to where you think you'll work. If you find the answer is three hours with four bus changes, you might want to reconsider.

If you plan to buy a car, exercise the same amount of caution as you would in the UK. If you plan on purchasing something from the classified section of your local newspaper, BUYER BEWARE, as you will not be as clued up as you were back in Blighty. When viewing vehicles, feel free to drag your boss's wife's hairdresser along (or anyone else who can help you avoid being ripped off). Always ask for the car's logbook (or foreign equivalent) and if you can get a professional to give it the once over, do so.

If you are not used to driving on the 'wrong' side of the road, practise on quiet out-of-town streets and work inwards! If you're a bit nervous and there is someone who can take you out for a few trial runs, don't be shy; accept their kind offer. Or if no one is 'game', consider paying for a refresher lesson – just to get you up to speed. Swot up on foreign road signs before you hit the road. And to avoid losing your nerve, try not to leave it too long before you get behind the wheel.

MEDIA

Brits love reading their UK newspapers, even after they've moved overseas. But while it's only natural to want to keep an eye on what's going on 'back there', you also need to fully absorb yourself in YNH's current affairs as well. For example, don't just buy national newspapers, get hold of the local community rag too. OK, so details of the church's garage sale might not make for the most scintillating read, but flicking through these newspapers can clue you up on neighbourhood news, social events and local concerns which can always be a route towards making new friends, buying a second-hand washing machine or learning to Salsa.

Another favourite of British nationals is the BBC World Service. The good old Beeb continues to transmit to record audiences around the world.[2] At the last count, it was 183 million (three times the UK population, amazingly) in 32 different languages! But, as with your newspaper reading, don't just listen to Auntie when it comes to tuning in. Try YNH's national and local radio stations too. Talkback shows can be real eye (or rather ear) openers for starters, as they give you an idea of what the great unwashed in YNH are fired up about. Watch television (obviously news and current affairs programmes will be a tad more educational than subtitled re-runs of *Only Fools and Horses*). All forms of media are going to help you brush up on the general knowledge of YNH. Be it politics or showbiz goss (often jolly similar in content), knowing who's done what or whom also provides good 'water-cooler discussion fodder' when you're trying to make friends at work. It's finding your common ground.

A few nights in front of the box will give you a helpful insight into what makes the masses tick. Whether it's Canada's answer to *EastEnders* or a Greek version of *Corrie*, you'll start discovering YNH's sense of humour too. And don't forget that media watching can also help you get to grips with a second language. Just don't get square eyes.

WILDLIFE

Whether it's mozzies in your bedroom, cockroaches in your cornflakes or pythons in your pool, there could be a few changes on the 'animal front' now that you've moved away from GB.

Some Sensible Girls who have moved to faraway lands like Africa or Australia will have to deal with the surreal possibility of being eaten by their local wildlife!

Rather than freak yourself out about the new assortment of God's creatures now living in your backyard, listen to what the neighbours say on such matters. They've lived with these critters all their lives and you don't see them jumping on a chair every time a spider strolls past. They should be able to help you differentiate between what's a genuine danger and what's just a little annoying. Who knows, they might be able to teach you a few tricks – how to remove lizards from your mailbox, bats from your belfry or alligators from your Zen water feature.

CULTURE

One of the largest hurdles that Sensible Girls have to leap over once they emigrate, is dealing with culture shock. Depending on where YNC is located (and how its cultural background differs from where you lived in the UK), this can range from feeling like a pin-prick in the finger to a sledgehammer in the back of the head. That said, the success of your assimilation into YNC can greatly depend on how YOU personally deal with the cultural differences presented to you. Remember, you are in control.

Margaret Malewski, author of *GenXpat*, has lived in a number of countries and experienced a variety cultures as a result. She believes that culture shock is not simply reacting to dress codes and religion, but that it is more complex an issue which forms the foundation of how you settle in to YNC:

'Culture shock occurs when you are taken out of your usual environment and the change makes you aware of how much you assume in your daily behaviour, in the same way that the absence of air would make you conscious of your need to breathe.'[3]

You suddenly realise how much you took for granted back in the UK and how much knowledge you have gathered over the years about how 'life worked'. Now you feel like you don't have a clue. But in order to settle in, you must start from the beginning and learn how YNC 'works'.

Sadly, there are a few Brits out there who don't quite 'get' the idea of assimilating into a new culture. Rather than slipping into a new life abroad, they try to recreate an exact replica of what they left behind – a Little Britain, if you will. It is often in such areas, which have a high concentration of British expats, that assimilation into the local culture gets overlooked and as a result resentment builds between foreigners (that's us) and locals (that's them). The irony of the situation is highlighted further when you get to know the type of people who are cocooning themselves in these micro-societies. They usually make up that small percentage of the population who left the UK moaning that 'it's overrun with immigrants who can't speak a word of English'. These people merrily plonk themselves in the Costa-del-Wherever and march into the nearest British pub to watch The Footy while supping a pint of Pride. Oh, and they do the whole thing while speaking a foreign language called English.

CHA!

Coming in at number two on our Top Ten Emigration Destinations for girls, Spain is one of the main countries that experience these British micro-societies which seem to be popping up all over the shop. We all know about the Costa del Sol, but did you know that there is a pretty village in the hills outside Malaga that, last count, had one British resident to every four Spaniards.[4] (I won't tell you where it is – as we might end up making it one in three.) Yikes!

Of course, one of the obvious ways of coping with culture shock is to find other Brits and stick together. After all, it's a relief when you're struggling with a new language or lifestyle. I have already sung the praises of expat communities and I will do so again in the next chapter. But there is a big difference between integrating into YNC's society while socialising with expats, and not mixing with anyone other than Bob and Jean in the King's Head, who 'can't be doing with any of that foreign muck'. Understand that this is nothing to do with who these people are or where they come from, it is simply about showing some respect for their new country to learning what it has to offer. As my Sensible Grandma would say 'everything in moderation', and that's the sensible way to treat the expat community in YNH. The aim is to get the right balance and enjoy their company, without completely blinkering oneself to everything else. It's about tolerance and consideration.

Margaret Malewski explains:[5] 'It is very important to discover the values that the members of a given culture hold, as these are the key to understanding, interpreting and anticipating the people's behaviour.'

You have to appreciate that you're in 'their' country now and it's up to you to take the first step towards integration. But once you've understood YNC's culture, Margaret believes you will be rewarded in more ways than one:

'Going through it [a culture shock] successfully can be very rewarding, through, as you end up with a more integrated and consciously held outlook on the world, which results in greater self-confidence and maturity.'

And let's face it – that can't be a bad thing, can it?

Culture shock can throw up even more challenging issues: your skin might be a different colour to everyone else living in YNH; your westernised social skills might be called into question; a foreign language could limit your understanding of YNC's new culture or you might well have to take on a new religion or dress code.

Over the past few years, UK attitudes towards certain dress codes seem to have gone a bit mental. Everyone has become hysterical about what is and isn't acceptable. This book is not the appropriate place to start debating such contentious issues, so instead I will leave you with my experience of visiting a Mature Sensible Girl who emigrated to Malaysia (a primarily Muslim country) six years ago.

Karen had emigrated (with her husband) to the outskirts of Kuala Lumpur and I was staying with them for a few nights, en route home to my Great Red Continent. If was a hot evening and we were getting ready to go out for dinner, so I asked Karen what I should (and shouldn't) wear. She looked at what I had on (a vest T-shirt and jeans – neither of which was too figure hugging or skimpy) and told me to make sure the tops of my shoulders were covered and my bra straps didn't poke out.

Simple.

I don't quite know what I had expected her to say (hijab, mackintosh and balaclava maybe?), but I suddenly realised that even the most Sensible of girls can get things a bit wrong sometimes. Either we get our baps out on the beach and wonder why there's a line of hairy men staring at us, or we over-compensate for what we don't fully understand and start looking like a *Star Wars* stand-in for Obi-Wan-Kenobi. Remember that you're not trying to change your culture, you're just respectfully adapting to YNC's.

And if you keep that in mind – you should be fine!

CHAPTER 19

HOMESICKNESS

Homesickness is a bit like seasickness.
You don't know how awful it is until you get it, and when you do,
it hits you right in the top of the stomach and you want to die.
ROALD DAHL[1]

OK, so Mr Dahl might have experienced a particularly severe
bout of homesickness to feel like he 'wanted to die', but there's
no disputing the fact that feeling homesick and missing loved
ones was a BIG concern when you were deciding whether you
wanted to emigrate or not. Remember the figures: 47 per cent of
British females surveyed said that missing family and friends
would actually prevent them from leaving Blighty in the first
place.[2] Well, you've left – but you're not out of the woods yet. The
stats show that in one year alone 91,000 British nationals
returned from living abroad,[3] back to the UK, and while I'm not
for one moment suggesting that all of them did so because they
felt homesick, focus groups revealed that Brits overwhelmingly
return to The Motherland because they miss loved ones. So how
does a Sensible Girl avoid giving up and going 'home'?

Coping with homesickness plays a *big* part in settling down.
You may have *physically* left the UK, but you might not have done
so *emotionally*. And in these formative months of your emigration,
you are particularly vulnerable to having a nasty attack of
homesickness. Roald Dahl's comparison to seasickness is good,
but maybe a female-friendly version might be a bit more
appropriate.

Homesickness is like going on a permanent holiday with PMT. It's unpredictable, it's moody, symptoms can vary greatly depending on the destination (and type of Sensible Girl that you are) and it can completely ruin things if it gets out of hand, both for you and anyone else who is around you. One minute you're smugly loving the fact that it's 35 degrees in the shade...and the next, you're sobbing over a subtitled episode of *The Bill*. You're all over the shop!

Homesickness looks something like this:

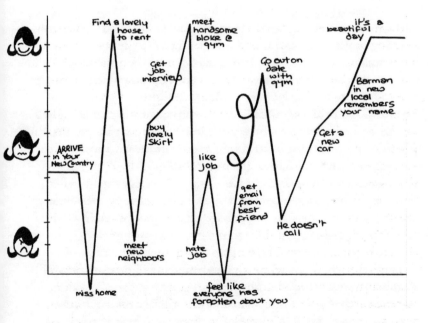

But when you shove its rather unpleasant, spiky form under the microscope for further analysis, what *is* homesickness?

'Homesickness is the result of extreme change,' says Lisa, our resident counselling psychologist.[4] 'Such a change does have an influence on our identity, the person who we think we are. When everything that reminds us of ourselves is removed, it's like we have to start all over again, discovering ourselves through our own eyes. It's like the old onion analogy: all the layers are kind of stripped away and we are left with the core of who we are and how we cope with the world. It's very confronting!'

The change that emigration hits us with is all-encompassing. It touches every aspect of our lives. Most Sensible Girls (who have not emigrated) usually get to deal with big changes individually, lining them up, one at a time. Whereas the change that you're currently trying to get your head round is big and sudden. Everything, both mental and physical, has just changed. From your house, job and circle of friends to the jam you spread on your toast in the morning. In one fell swoop. BANG – everything is different.

William Bridges,[5] author of *Transitions: Making Sense of Life's Changes*, believes that there are three stages of change, which when applied to the subject of emigration, clearly illustrate the emotional shift Sensible Girls must undergo:

'Endings are the first phrase of transition [leaving home]. The second phase is a time of lostness and emptiness [homesickness] before life resumes an intelligible pattern and direction, while the third phase is that of beginning anew [settling in].'

How quickly and efficiently you move from 'stage one' to 'stage three' will pretty much determine how homesickness will affect your new life abroad.

Some changes will be positive, some will be negative, but when you emigrate it's less a case of identifying which is which and more a case of coping with the sheer volume of change, which can often be overwhelming. Change is a funny thing. When we don't have it, we moan about being bored and crave it.* But when we eventually get it, we can often freak out and want to dash back to our original circumstances, where we felt the safety of familiarity. This might be do-able when returning a poorly chosen pair jeans...but less so when changing one's mind about moving overseas.

Changes created by living abroad become even more potent because of their 'unknown qualities'. In emigrating, you have willingly removed yourself from a secure, quantifiable, 'known' life and transported yourself, under considerable stress, into an unknown one. And that can cause even more angst, because until you know what you're actually dealing with, you can't fully stand up to it.

So now we're getting an idea of how miserable you really feel – what are we going to do about it?

Psychologists can offer up a number of mental exercises and checklists to help alleviate some of the symptoms of homesickness. 'Work out what it is that you are really missing,' suggests Lisa.

---

* Remember sitting on that bus and staring out the window, daydreaming of emigrating?

'Sometimes the experience of homesickness is that we are simply sad or grieving our old life back home. We cannot put it down to one specific reason or person. Note that homesickness is normal and expected. Allow yourself to feel it and be compassionate to yourself about it. The attitude you have towards yourself makes all the difference.'[6]

A recent UK newspaper article, giving advice to Brits planning to move abroad, summed things up nicely (albeit harshly):

'Know that the unfamiliarity of daily life will initially overwhelm and depress you.'[7]

Firm but fair, I'm sure you'll agree. But if you can appreciate that this, to some degree, will affect how you settle down in YNH, you'll come out 'the other side' a lot quicker.

BE PREPARED

Imagine that your particular strain of homesickness is a boxing opponent. One who may challenge you to a 'mental punch-up' at any time. In order to deal with such a threat, you need to exercise your brain, to mentally train and be ready to face up to this cerebral bully-boy whenever necessary.

Prepare yourself for the changes that lie ahead (and the ones you are starting to encounter already). You will have already done a lot of mental preparation before leaving the UK where you undoubtedly worked though your worries and imagined what you were going to encounter upon arriving in YNH. Keep up that visualisation, keep thinking ahead and anticipating what the next change is going to be. That way, if homesickness does throw down the gauntlet, you can smash its face in.

ACCEPTANCE

First of all, trust your judgement and accept that you made these scary life changes for good reason. People change jobs, get extreme haircuts or split up from partners, because they believe it's the 'right decision'. And emigrating was the right decision for you. Doubting yourself is only sabotaging your chances of getting on with things.

Once you accept your decision to emigrate, you need to accept the changes that have arisen as a result.

'No, you can't speak the language fluently yet', or 'Yes, you do have to make new friends' – but all of these changes are inevitable if you are to succeed in settling down in YNH. Learning to accept them will, to some degree, be like going through the grieving process that Lisa has already mentioned. You feel the loss of your leaving your old life behind, but you will eventually feel the benefits of accepting your new one.

Life coach Lesley also believes that being open to new ideas, people and information (i.e. your new life) will help you accept the change:

'Homesickness sucks. You just need to enjoy all the newness and treat this experience as a blank canvas on to which you can paint any picture you want. Give yourself the freedom and permission to be brave, daring and adventurous. Give yourself permission to try out new things and allow yourself to make mistakes. Be accepting and try not to compare your old life, with your new. Thinking things like, "we wouldn't have done that at home" merely sets you apart and doesn't help with integration.'[8]

Sabina and Nynke, our expat coaches, agree:

'You will never ever find what you've left behind, so don't hold on to it. In order to achieve happiness it is better to understand that you have to adapt to the new situation rather than having set expectations that you have to adjust all the time.'[9]

In other words, accepting the change involves a certain amount of flexible thinking.

BE POSITIVE

An obvious suggestion, but one that life coach Lesley believes is the key to dealing with homesickness.

'Try to embrace your new life experience with open arms. Remember, you have the resources within you to do anything you want. If you've been brave enough to take this huge step then you will make it!'[10]

There is a lot of literature out there on positive thinking. *Secret* books and DVDs, banging on about 'putting it out there and asking the universe for peace, love and a big wad of cash'. Whether you are a 'believer' or not is unimportant, because all we are dealing with here is appreciating the benefit of positive thought. The notion that you can enjoy your emigration, embrace it even. Face up to the challenge and take pride in the fact that you're achieving new goals, both large and small, every single day. Keeping an optimistic outlook reduces your fear of failure, which in turn pushes you on to even greater achievements.

COMMUNICATE

Andrea Martins, co-founder of the expat women's support website ExpatWomen.com[11] makes an interesting observation in that, until you have emigrated yourself, it's very easy to focus on the 'exciting and privileged assignments abroad' and forget about the fact that you've just sacrificed pretty much all of your support systems back in Blighty; 'extended family, friends, babysitters, medical specialists, counsellors, business contacts, sports teams, hobby clubs – literally everyone that you would usually turn to for help'. And in leaving all of these good people behind, 'going abroad necessitates the need to set up all of these critical support networks again'.

It can be a vicious circle, but the fact that you don't have friends and family to support you in YNH makes you need them more than ever. But with communications as developed (and relatively inexpensive) as they now are, there's no excuse if you feel miserable. Tell someone! Don't keep things bottled up.

People back home may not even realise what you are going through. After all, if the only communication they've had from you is a 'what's on your mind' Facebook update boasting about the weather, they're hardly going to be sending out the Search and Rescue party are they?

'It's important to remain connected with people from our past,'[12] says counselling psychologist Lisa. Phoning home and having a proper chat with someone who knows you, is a real pick-me-up. But it is also important to start connecting with people who will form your future network of friends in YNH.

Author and expat expert Robin Pascoe points out that in 'the old days', friend networks would have primarily been based around 'bricks and mortar' meaning that you had to physically go and visit a club, gym or social gathering. But thanks to the Internet, virtual support networks, expat clubs and the like are much easier to access and an invaluable tool when settling in.[13]

STAY HEALTHY

An obvious one, but often overlooked. Margaret Malewski's research in *GenXpat* revealed that many expats reported needing up to 12 hours of sleep a night during their first couple of weeks of settling in.[14] Which is a good indicator of how exhausting the process can be.

How can you hope to successfully settle in to YNH if you're not sleeping properly, eating properly or are just generally feeling rundown? As any doctor will tell you, once you're physically low, your mental state follows and homesickness pries its way in and starts bashing you about. So keep yourself in tip-top condition by eating well, exercising, relaxing properly and trying to relieve stress wherever possible. And as they say...don't forget to breathe!

DON'T BE AFRAID TO ASK FOR HELP

Expat coaches (two of whom have been dishing out sensible advice throughout this book) are a very sensible way of successfully settling in to life abroad. Expat coaches Nynke and Sabina explain why talking to an expert[†] can help:

'When you leave your home country, you leave behind everything that acknowledges you and gives you confidence. As a result you have to build this up from scratch in your new country. To be able to do this we work on self development with our clients, supporting them to find their own ways to gain confidence again.'[15]

Sensible Girls should be able to find out whether their new country has a coaching service by checking on local expat websites or local directories. And don't forget, you can always receive coaching remotely if need be (**www.theexpatcoaches.com**).

Sometimes homesickness can be hard to shake off and left unattended can develop into something a little bit more sinister. It can even be a trigger for other, low-lying psychological issues that have been lurking undetected for years. If you find things start to get ugly, stop struggling and go and have a chat with a professional counsellor. It may be something you never imagined doing, but it's not a sign of weakness and it will make you feel much better.

OK, so that was heavy. But don't panic. For most people, homesickness is more of an annoyance than a debilitating ailment, and dealing with it can be as simple as having a nice chat with your mum.

---

† Indeed an experienced expert expat!

It won't take long for your mum and dad to start asking lots of questions when you phone home and if the issue of homesickness arises, they might even try the sneaky 'well you can always come home' comment, which although well intentioned, doesn't really help your cause. They will quiz you on whether you've found a good job yet, whether you've got somewhere nice to live or whether you've met your future husband (if you're a Single Gal). Meanwhile, you're still trying to work out how to use the local bus timetable or avoid getting pickled octopus when you ask for a pack of ciggies at the local supermarket.

Unfortunately it is very difficult for them to fully appreciate what you're experiencing at the moment. You can try to explain to them that you're currently scaling the world's largest learning curve. Or that it is about the 'little things' as much as the 'big ones', but if you are hoping for them to fully comprehend what you're currently going through...they won't. Because unless they've emigrated themselves,‡ they can't.

---

‡ And let's assume they haven't, otherwise you'd have a dual passport and would not be reading this book.

Sure they can empathise, offer encouragement down the phone, and try to help you cope with all the change in your life. But they can't fully appreciate every nuance of your migration. However, there is a new network of potential friends out there who do appreciate what you're going through, who do understand and who want to help – and they are our good old friends, the expats.

BRITS ABROAD

Now we've already mentioned the expat community in both a positive and negative light over the last few chapters, but when it comes to homesickness, having a chat with an expat (albeit a sensible one) can go to the top of your 'things to do' list. Even though Brits abroad are renowned for displaying strong emotional connections with the Motherland, they are a surprisingly positive bunch for having left it.[§]

As Kath Woodward, author of *Understanding Identity*,[16] explains:

'Identities are more often constructed in relation to the place we have come from than the place we might be going to.'

[§] In fact, far more so than when they were actually living in the UK!

Which seems to explain why a lot of Sensible Expats, have stronger feelings of national identity once they move overseas, i.e. they wouldn't have been seen dead waving a Union Jack in the UK, but in Their New Country they're painting their faces red, white and blue every time an international sporting event kicks off.

Feeling irrationally patriotic (otherwise known as GB Sickness – we'll get to that in Chapter 21) is part and parcel of homesickness. However, if you are feeling a bit negative about YNH (otherwise known as Country Fatigue), Sensible Expats will set you straight. In fact, you're in danger of not being able to shut them up!

Talking to Brits abroad is helpful on many levels and raises some very interesting observations. For example, when researching this book, I sent out a questionnaire to a number of Sensible Girls who had emigrated across the globe. One of the first things I noticed was less to do with what they were saying, but rather how they were saying it. They were all such chatterboxes! They had this remarkable desire to share their emigrating experiences. It was almost like a catharsis; a pooling of knowledge. These expats opened up to reveal quite intimate feelings and emotions that probably wouldn't have been disclosed if we had been talking about every day life back in the UK.

At first I couldn't explain their candour, but after conversing with these Escape Artists for some time, I realised that they had opened up because they know how difficult emigrating can be to begin with. But they also know how great it is once you get settled in.

Counselling psychologist Lisa explains:

'This is "universality". When people get together, the disclosure of personal information regarding common experiences is something that creates a sense of trust and safety. It's really very therapeutic and reminds us that we are not alone in this world,'[17] which is important, because when we're trying to fight off a severe case of homesickness, we often need reminding that we're not alone!

Being an expat is like belonging to an exclusive member's only club. You have to have 'done it' to be in it.

So, if reading this chapter helps you feel a bit better because you now belong to a brand new club with members all around the world, imagine how helpful it would be to meet a few of these people. To chat to them, to find out how they feel about living in the nether regions of the globe. To ask them whether they got homesick and whether they thought about jacking it all in... because the chances are they did!

Even though these brave pioneers crossed oceans and continents to seek a better life, enduring heartache, stress, upheaval and whatever else the Emigration Fairy lobbed at them, they still remain wonderfully positive when recounting their travelling tales. And THAT is a very important point for your 'newly-emigrated-little-mind' to grasp.

Don't be mistaken into thinking that your move to YNH has been any harder than theirs because, with present-day communications and travel being so accessible, it probably won't have been. The key point here is that they're looking back on their emigration. They've donned those fantastical rose-tinted glasses and had time to settle down...and that's exactly what you need to give yourself now – time.

USE THE 'P' WORD

Knowing that you need patience in order to settle into your emigration is one thing. Finding it is another. After all, the sheer volume of change you're coping with at the moment automatically makes you impatient. You want to feel happy and settled in your new life – and you want to feel it NOW!

Too bad, because patience is an absolute pre-requisite when it comes to dealing with homesickness. Having only just arrived, you can't rush things and you can't project how you're feeling right now on to how you're going to feel in another week, month or year.

Of course you will always miss loved ones, but you will adjust to not having them around you all the time. Having just ripped yourself from one existence and plonked yourself down in to a completely alien one, you're still acclimatising and you can't expect these feelings to change overnight. Your poor brain has been in overdrive for the past few intense months, plotting every detail of this move, so it's very difficult to switch off and stop analysing everything. This all sounds like common sense now, but for those of you who lie awake in the dark, worrying, getting upset, fearing that you've made a terrible mistake, you know that common sense doesn't always make an appearance on such occasions.

I promise it will get easier. It just takes time!

AVOID THE 'F' WORD

Forever is a very scary word for recently emigrated Sensible Young Ladies.

Now that you're embarking on a brand new life, it's only natural to start asking questions, some of which are more constructive than others: How am I ever going to make friends? What job should I apply for? Where do I want to live? But camouflaged in their midst, feigning innocence and pretending to be useful, is a question that can really freak you out:

Am I going to stay here **forever**?

Noooooooooooooooooooooooooooooooooooooooooooooooooo ooooooooooooo!

Never

EVER

use the 'F' word.

'Nothing is forever,' says counselling psychologist Lisa. 'It's how we live moment by moment that counts and futurising and trying to see how the future looks, only creates more anxiety and stress. Don't go there!'[18]

Talk to any Sensible Girl who has been living abroad for a substantial amount of time and even they will have difficulty including the 'F' word in a sentence. It's just too tricky – too loaded. You might live in YNH for six months or 60 years. But you can't possibly know that yet. You've just got to keep your options open and let's face it, your options have just increased BIG TIME, since emigrating.

Back home, if someone had asked you what your plans were five years ago, you probably wouldn't have predicted *this*. So stop trying to predict what's going to happen next in YNH. You don't have a crystal ball, and neither does anyone else, so you'll just have to wait and see.

ROUTINE

Essentially you need to get busy and distract yourself, to throw yourself headlong into the exciting business of settling down. You need to fill up your days and nights so there is simply no time for negative thinking. It's all about finding some kind of routine. That word may conjure up flashbacks of the 'British routine' you worked so hard to get out of, but not all routine is bad.

We are all, to some degree, creatures of habit. So going to the same restaurant every Friday evening and becoming a regular (which, as you know from the previous chapter, will give you a nice sense of belonging and help you settle down) is a routine, just not a dull one! Routine and repetition are also useful when it comes to meeting people. For example, if you go to the gym at the same time every day, you'll probably see the same people. And if you like the look of any of these fellow fitness fanatics, get chatting: they could be potential chums.

Some escape artists, especially Sensible Families who are negotiating their way through more than one person's set of 'homesickness issues', may find themselves so wrapped up in organising a new life that they forget to schedule in a bit of fun. So the minute you have some form of stability, don't be afraid to put a few treats back in the diary. It may be a visit to a museum or a picnic in the park, but whatever it is, having something to look forward to certainly takes your mind off what you're missing.

Settling in to your new job, working out which beach you like to walk the dog on, learning where the best fruit and veg shop is...all of these experiences join together to build up your new (and improved) routine, otherwise known as Your New Life. The more you learn about YNH the more knowledge and confidence you have to enable you to start fitting in...and before you know it, you won't be the new girl any more.

A recent survey revealed that 92 per cent of British nationals living overseas said they were 'happier living abroad than they were in the UK'[19] and in another survey, more than half said that they would not swap their lifestyle and climate for that of Britain.[20] So it's not all that bad – you WILL get over your bout of homesickness and you WILL start enjoying your brand new life. According to Margaret Malewski,[21] 'The secret to happiness abroad, and perhaps in general, is wanting what you have, rather than missing what you have not got.' So make a real effort to focus on the good things.

The last question I put to my trusty emigration advisory board was 'What would you say to anyone who is considering moving abroad?' and the unanimous answer was to go for it. Not one person said anything about having regrets, not even the ones who have since moved back to the UK. A Sensible Young Lady called Erica, who emigrated to Switzerland summarised things beautifully, so I will leave you in her capable hands (or should I say words):

'Naturally, I do miss a lot of things about the UK, primarily my friends and family. However, if I were to be completely honest with myself, life would not be the same if I went back to London now. Five years on, most of my friends have taken the plunge and moved. Some still live in the UK and a few, like myself, have ventured overseas. I find it sometimes difficult to accept that the world has moved on, even though my memories prefer to keep things just as they were before I left. I never regret being one of the first to take that big step and make these changes in my life and I feel proud that maybe others were not quite as brave as I was!'[22]

CHAPTER 20

THE PERKS: REASONS TO
BE CHEERFUL

Change is inevitable...except from a vending machine.
ANON

This chapter is all about accentuating the positive (and slightly silly) points that have floated to the surface since you arrived on foreign shores. After all, you've not hoiked yourself all the way to YNH for a load of old cobblers and a perma-tan...so here's the good stuff to watch out for.*

1.   Black bogie elimination

---

* Where you've emigrated to will dictate how many of the following pick-me-ups you encounter. But fear not, there's something for all the family in this top ten.

Euwww. Always a crowd pleaser! If you're lucky enough to move out of a smelly British city to somewhere a bit cleaner, you will notice the difference. Less time spent underground or in traffic jams, less pollution, less smoky parties, more open spaces, more fresh air, more time spent in the great outdoors.

Blow your nose...examine...and enjoy!

2. Big adventure

So far, there is very little that is predictable about life in YNH and, although this can be exhausting and unnerving (see Chapter 19, Homesickness), it can also very exciting. Cast your mind back to life in GB and I'm guessing that everything was planned, scheduled and accounted for. Yawn.

Now, the world is your oyster and your new life is the shiny pearl rolling around inside it, so 'boring' should not even figure in your vocabulary. You haven't had the chance to limit yourself by developing mental boundaries yet, you're finding yourself, as much as finding your way around...so while everything is fresh and exciting, get out into that big, new, wide world of yours and explore!

3. Your re-invention tour

In YNH nobody really knows you. They know nothing of your political preferences or embarrassing habits and they've NOT heard the story about when you vomited out of a taxi window on THAT Hen Do in Brighton.

So you see as a grown-up Sensible† Young Lady, this is a rare situation to find yourself in and one that you should enjoy (and maybe even exploit a little), because as far as anyone in YNH is concerned – you're brand new!

---

† Almost!

You are lucky enough to be able to wipe your slate clean and start again. At this stage of the game you have no enemies, no bad press and no scandalous rumours. Pure as the driven snow (or so it seems) – so let's keep it that way and give yourself a mental and physical revamp.

And, speaking of revamps, if you dig out that crumpled old Wish List you wrote all those months ago, weren't you thinking of giving yourself a career revamp once you arrived in YNH? Your daydreams of retraining to become a graphic designer/scuba diver/aromatherapist could well be within your grasp, so now is the time to explore these possibilities.

I must point out that putting a bit of 'spin' on yourself in the quest for re-invention is one thing; pretending to be Mick Jagger's estranged love child is another. Elaborate and exaggerate, but don't lie. It's not nice and, more importantly, you will get found out. And then nobody will want to play with you.

4. Cold turkey

It doesn't sound like much of a perk – but it is.

While we're on the subject of re-invention and self-improvement, is there anything that you do, that you wish you didn't? For example, might you enjoy the odd cigarette?

Whether you smoke, eat too much chocolate, drink too much wine or fall for lousy blokes, now would be a very sensible time to stop, as you have just officially broken free from every single routine your old life had to offer. Which means that for the moment, we can assume nothing in YNH can truly be associated with your old bad habits.

Of course, the devil on your shoulder will be whispering in your ear that 'emigrating is stressful and you need that nicotine fix'.‡ But take it from someone who was bessies with the Marlboro Man for a good few years before giving him the flick upon reaching my Great Red Continent. If you have any inclination whatsoever to give up, take advantage of your virginal status and make the changes before you begin to build up new routines.

Bad habits can be broken as part of your re-invention. New exercise regimes and healthy eating programmes can become part of your new life the same way learning a second language can. It just takes an extra bit of willpower.

5. Bilingual baby

You may not be fluent, but your language skills are bound to be improving. You probably don't realise how much of the lingo you're absorbing on a daily basis. Of course this is something you are going to have to work at. But it will be a great new skill once you've cracked it – and it's going to impress the hell out of your friends back in Blighty!

6. Selfish cow!

So, back home you had a collection of fab friends and a matching social calendar, whereas now that you've moved abroad that diary might be looking a bit sparse. Don't be glum. As with all things in life (especially in emigration) there's a definite trade-off here. Put it another way: before you emigrated, how many times

---

‡ Chocolate mud-cake/carafe of Chianti (insert vice here).

did you have to go to something because you felt obliged to. Be it work commitments or pressure from your girlfriends, those kind of social obligations no longer exist. You are your own boss...in charge of your own Friday Night Destiny.

You will be, of course, making all sorts of new friends and partying arrangements, but this time round you'll be 100 per cent in control. If you want to do tequila slammers with your new next door neighbours – do it. If you don't, there is nobody to justify your actions to, no one to judge and no best-friend-protocol to negotiate. In short, you can bloody well please yourself. Start as you mean to go on.

7.   Beauty flash balm
Sunshine (in moderation of course), improved eating habits, fewer later nights, more exercise, fresh air, less stress and a healthy portion of Cold Turkey.

Watch your makeover unfold before your very eyes. If you could pot what your skin is currently enjoying, you'd give Estée and Elizabeth a run for their money.

Sweetie, emigrating is definitely good for you – you're looking gorgeous!

8.   Emigration agoraphobia
You probably weren't presented with the opportunity to have a crack at agrophobia back in the UK – claustrophobia maybe, but open spaces aren't exactly ten-a-penny in suburban Britain!

One of the top reasons for emigrating is in order to find an improved standard of living – i.e. giving your urban rabbit hutch the heave-ho and finding a bit of breathing space. That may come in the form of an extra bedroom in your new apartment or 40 hectares of farmland to grow your carrots, but either way, your claustrophobic days are over.

These wide open spaces that lie before you are not just limited to 'the physical'. Oh no – your narrow little mind has just been liberated as well. Back in Blighty the suffering Rat-Racers are still stuck in their ruts, working hideously long hours (the most in Europe) and yet taking teeny-tiny amounts of annual leave. So while you are co-ordinating your re-invention in YNH, appreciate the fact that you might just get a few more hours to yourself each week – and maybe even a few more days at the beach each year too.

9.   Men perks (if you already have a man)

You were warned at the beginning of this book that emigrating was tough and if your relationship wasn't solid, things might get a bit messy. True enough.

But now that you're settling down in YNH I'll let you into a little secret. Leaving all of your friends and family behind and grabbing YNH by the horns can also do wonders for your relationship.

'My boyfriend and I found that emigration really brought us closer together,' says Sensible Girl Joanne who emigrated to Australia. 'After all, you can't have a row and run off to your mum's or mate's house. Out here, you only have each other. In the UK we had separate hobbies and social lives, whereas here we're hoping to do more things together.'[1] A large number of couples who move abroad talk of how they 'pull together' once they are faced with all the challenges emigration presents. Whether it's a simple case of 'them and us' or a newly discovered reliance on each other, analysis is not necessary, a united front is!

10. Men perks (if you left a man behind...or simply want a new one)

Whether he was a Reluctant Partner who didn't come up with the goods, or just an old-fashioned chump, never doubt yourself. You did the right thing by leaving him behind.

And now that you're starting your brand new life with a nice new selection of boys to choose from, aren't you pleased you did? It's amazing what you can achieve when you take a step outside your comfort zone. A change of scenery and suddenly there are potential suitors wherever you look. It's the emigrating formula to meet Mr Right.

$$\text{EMIGRATING} \times \frac{\text{NEW COUNTRY}}{\text{NEW OPPORTUNITIES}} = \frac{\text{NEW MAN /}}{\text{NEW ROMANCE}}$$

So, you see, it's not all doom and gloom. Yes, homesickness is horrid and no, emigrating isn't going to be easy, but the positives outweigh the negatives, wouldn't you agree?

CHAPTER 21

POST-EMIGRATING AILMENTS

Patriotism is the conviction that your country is superior to all others
...because you were born in it.
GEORGE BERNARD SHAW[1]

OK, so after months of exposure you're now immune to the wide range of pre-emigrating ailments that dogged you in the run up to your UK departure.

Now it's time to settle into phase two of your emigration, as you try to acclimatise to your new home. Sadly, there are a number of 'bugs' that you cannot be inoculated against and these can often be the cause of your 'bad day in paradise'.

HOMESICKNESS
We've already spent a lot of time on this one – so feel free to revisit Chapter 19 when necessary.

GB SICKNESS

Symptoms This has similarities with homesickness, but you find yourself pining for 'things' rather than people. You forget all the reasons why you left the UK and concentrate on soft focus images of country pubs, roast dinners and the designer bag section in Harvey Nichols. These rose-tinted reminiscences (which always seem to be accompanied by a rousing rendition of 'Land of Hope and Glory'), can develop into a psychotic form of patriotism when abroad.

Cure In a recent survey,[2] 62 per cent of Brits who had recently emigrated cited 'dissatisfaction with the UK' as the reason for moving. But for some odd reason (that we've already touched upon in Chapter 19) Brits abroad become far more patriotic when they're...well...abroad. If trying to give your GB sickness the old heave-ho, you need a reality check, so e-mail one of your old UK workmates and find out what the latest office gossip is. I guarantee that it's the 'same old crap'!

And I bet it's raining too!

FSD: FASHION SENSE DISPLACIA

Symptoms   Just because everyone else appears to be wearing scandalous crimes-of-fashion in YNH, it does not give you the excuse to embrace these new looks. While doing as the Romans do should usually be encouraged, mullets, terry-towelling socks, and baggy New Age T-shirts with dolphins on should be AVOIDED.

Cure   Our fashion guru Oonagh Brennan acknowledges this can be tricky. 'It's easy to lose your sense of style when you move abroad, even if you were a bit of a fashionista back home. Things are different, you're out of your familiar climate (which might mean showing a little more flesh than you're used to), you don't have your friends to influence and advise you and you might not have access to the shops that the UK's bigger cities offered.'

That said, you still need to get a grip on the situation (especially if you are Sensible, Single and on the prowl for a new gentleman). Live by the following rule when it comes to your wardrobe: if you wouldn't wear it with your friends back in the UK, do not wear it in YNH. A lot of UK High Street Fashion Favourites now offer internet mail order but in the meantime get yourself an emergency overseas subscription to one of the British glossies and read carefully!

DODGY THERMOSTAT

Symptoms   Bloody 'ell it's hot.*

You wanted sun, but this is ridiculous. Just sitting still makes you sweat, the simple act of breathing makes you lightheaded and complaining about the weather makes you feel positively nauseous. What's a Sensible Girl to do?

Cure   You wouldn't be a true Brit abroad if you didn't complain about the weather. Aircon, factor 30 and a cold shower – or a radiator, thermal undies and a hot bath.

---

* You may be required to replace 'hot' with 'cold', depending on locality of YNH to the equator.

It's called acclimatising and you'll get the hang of it...eventually!

HE'S DRIVING YOU CRAZY!

Symptoms   Applies to Sensible Couples only.

You and your partner have been living in each other's pockets for a few months now and things are getting spiky. His sweet little quirks are starting to drive you mad. Your arguments are becoming more frequent, the results of which make you want to smash his face in (in a nice way of course). And, to make matters worse, you don't know a single sausage in Your New Neighbourhood who you can go and have a good old whinge to.

Cure   There isn't a cure and you don't need one. You just need a bit of space and a few more friendly people to talk to.

While we've already acknowledged that couples can grow stronger as a result of emigrating, there's still a very important need for the two of you to keep your own individuality. At first, socialising (especially if you're doing so in a foreign language) can be quite a daunting affair, so you'll probably end up doing most things together for the first few months, which is totally the norm with expat couples. But the best way to improve relationship issues and deal with a spot of cabin fever is to try to get out there and do your 'own thing' as soon as you feel brave enough (or just before!).

Aside from helping your relationship get back on track, it will give you a *huge* confidence boost

285

once you start finding your own friends, hobbies and space! So refer back to previous chapters regarding making new friends and settling in.

MISPLACED HUSBAND

Symptoms   Applies to Sensible Couples only.

You're a tailing spouse and you and your partner emigrated because of his work placement and now you're beginning to wonder why you bloody well bothered. He's working all the hours God sends and you never get to see him. Who cares if you're racking up the yen/dollars/euros – you're bored, lonely and feel like a Stepford Widow.

Cure   First of all, give him a bit of time to settle in. People who emigrate for work reasons experience a high level of pressure when starting a new job abroad and it's particularly important for our beloved Hunter Gatherers to get it right (it's a pride thing!). After all, making the job work will usually mean the difference between staying in YNC or having to move back to the UK, so it's only natural that your partner wants to impress the hell out of his new boss...and acquire a more secure future for you all in YNC.

But, if your partner is misplaced on an increasingly regular basis, you will need to sit down and have a proper grown-up chat. The key treatment for this ailment is communication and a little patience. But in the meantime, why not get a dog for company – often more reliable and easier to house-train.

SAME S**T…DIFFERENT COUNTRY

Symptoms   The clue's in the title.

Cure   There is no cure. Author of *GenXpat*, Margaret Malewski, wisely observes that you can 'exchange your society for one whose values more closely match yours, but no relocation can help you run way from your own inner conflicts.'[3] Or as our resident expat coaches Sabrina and Nynke put it: 'You take yourself with you wherever you go…you can't escape yourself.'[4]

Re-invention is one thing, trying to leave your past behind is another. So if you thought you could move to another country to lose your emotional baggage in transit – think again!

'IT'S A GLAND THING'

Symptoms   Yes, it's hard trying to find new friends, but they're not hiding in the cream cake counter at your local bakery, are they? A bowlful of calories is no substitute for a girlie chat, so step away from the tiramisu.

Cure   Instant gratification – dig out your cheap phone card, get on the blower and have a good old gossip with the girls.

Long-term gratification – join, enrol or learn something new and get out there and make some new friends! You can do it.

S.O.H. BYPASS

Symptoms   You can't see 'the joke' any more.

Cure   OK, even if everybody is beginning to annoy the tits off you, try to laugh along. We all know that 'foreign humour' is a slippery fish to get a grasp of. People often poke fun at the new girl and you'll be accepted a lot quicker if you can join in the fun, rather than storming off to the ladies loo in a strop.

Laughing at yourself is always a good ice-breaker no matter what country you're in. Laughing at them is possibly less acceptable (for the time being) so try laughing *with* them instead. And if their jokes are not particularly funny, you'll just have to brush up on your acting skills.

S.O.D. BYPASS

Symptoms   You can't seem to find your sense of direction either.

Whenever you set foot outside your front door you get lost and it's no good asking for directions because you just end up nodding idiotically while the helpful passer-by points wildly and talks so quickly, you can't understand a single word they're saying.

Cure   Everything is hard when you first emigrate, so the sooner you learn to try to stop stressing when things don't go exactly according to plan, the better. Ask any Expat how they got on when they first arrived in Their New Country, and they will confirm that 'getting lost' was a pastime. So unless you've got an appointment you're heading to, who cares. Go out and spend the entire day getting lost, because that's the only way to learn. Take yourself out on a Magical Mystery Tour (and invest in a foreign A–Z), and you'll be scooting around YNH before you know it!

POOR PAL PERFORMANCE

Symptoms   This applies to your friends back in the UK.

Your sister forgot your birthday and your best friend didn't bother to ask how your first job interview went last week. What's with everyone? Don't they understand what you're going through at the moment? Don't they care? Helloooo?

Cure   A Sensible Senior called Sheilagh, who has lived both in Africa and Australia, explained things very simply when I was lamenting about friends back 'home' who seemed to be drifting away and didn't seem to care anymore. 'At this moment in time,' she said, 'you need them more than they need you.'

No doubt all of your friends and family miss you terribly, but they are still living their same familiar lives and coping with all the usual hassles and stresses they dealt with when you were around. They're busy and they are secure in their circle of friends, their job, their house, they know what to expect when they wake up each morning and they know, pretty much, how their day is going to end.

You don't.

And this lack of familiarity is difficult to deal with, especially when your 'support group' of friends and family are not quite so readily available. It's not that they don't care, they just don't *know*. You begin to scrutinise your friends' behaviour. You start looking at things more closely because of distance. Why didn't they e-mail you straight back? Why haven't they remembered your birthday?

Be sensible and take the time to explain that you're feeling a bit disconnected after the Big Move. Don't forget that they've got dramas playing out in their lives too. They don't know what life is like for you in YNC. But if they are a good friend, they will listen and learn and make an extra effort to make you feel loved – even from afar.

VANISHING ACTS

Symptoms   This also applies to your friends back in the UK (who didn't make that extra effort!).

Having always believed that true friends remain true friends no matter where you live, you may find that a few people, whom you always assumed were mates for life, disappear into thin air.

Cure   Luckily, this emigrating ailment is pretty rare, especially seeing as there is no known cure. However, there is a natural 'balance' you should be aware of.

First of all, appreciate all of your true friends back in the Motherland – the ones who will always be there for you. Concentrate on them. Remember their birthdays, invite them to visit your new home and keep communications flowing.

As for the ones who don't bother, who can't manage a quick e-mail or phone call now and then, try not to get too glum. Sadly, a few relationships will not survive the pressures of distance. Some may be 'downsized' and some will simply vanish. Just try to be philosophical about the whole thing rather than getting too upset. Slowly but surely, substitute these Vanishing Acts with new work colleagues, people from your local taverna and next door neighbours. In other words, new friends. It evens out in the end.

HOLIDAY DEFICIENCY DISORDER

Symptoms   This is quite the opposite of Vanishing Acts.

Things are getting hectic. When you're not shepherding visiting loved ones around YNH, you're dashing back to Blighty attending yet another wedding or naming ceremony. All of this would be marvellous if your surname happened to be Onassis or Trump, but it's not and your bank balance doesn't match up either. Not to mention the dwindling amount of annual leave you have remaining. After a few months of this rather expensive long-distance socialising, you need a 'proper holiday'.

Cure   Having people visit you and actually see how your new life 'works' is psychologically very important.

It validates your emigration and gives you the opportunity to show everyone what you've achieved and why you wanted to achieve it in the first place.

But you'll start to realise that it's all or nothing when you first settle down in YNH. Nobody just pops round for a cuppa any more...it's the 'stay in the spare room for as long as you want' kind of visit these days. However, once people's curiosity has worn off, the volume of house guests will probably die down to a manageable trickle.

After the first couple of visits, when your friends have nosed around Your New Life abroad enough to give their stamp of approval, why not suggest meeting them in neutral territory next time? You could find a nice holiday destination equidistant between the two of you. That way, you don't have to waste all of your annual leave either trolling around the UK or playing tour guide in YNH and you can lounge on a lilo to your heart's desire.

ACCENT AFFECTATION

Symptoms   This bad habit manifests itself in three ways:

    i.   You develop a weird, hybrid accent – a Transatlantic Twang, a Continental Lisp or an Antipodean Inflection.

    ii. You have the reverse reaction and turn into the Queen, a 'Cockney Sparrah' or the regional equivalent.

    iii. You alternate between the two.

Cure   None of the above accents should be encouraged if you ever plan on returning to your native homeland and want to be taken seriously. If your best friend comments on how different you sound, next time you speak on the phone...TAKE NOTE.

PARALLEL UNIVERSE SYNDROME (PUS)

Symptoms   PUS usually lies dormant for at least 12 months while you're busy settling down in YNH and symptoms are mostly experienced when returning to the UK for a holiday.

Once you start moving around your old UK life again (which probably hasn't changed that much

293

since you left), you begin to realise that you are now the proud owner of TWO lives. A British one and a foreign one. Both are fully functioning, run simultaneously and you can seamlessly step, from one to the other.[†]

...MAGIC!

Cure   You need to get things from one life crossing over into the other. For example, once you've visited the UK a couple of times and your British chums learn more about your new life overseas, they will ask more specific questions about your new job, home, friends. Your New Foreign Life is seeping into your British one.

Likewise, if you have UK visitors come and stay with you in YNH, they will meet your foreign friends who will, in turn, learn more about what you were all like before you arrived in YNH. Your Old British Life is leaking into your Foreign One.

The more overlapping you can get between your two parallel universes, the less of a split personality you're likely to develop.

YOU'VE TRIED ABSOLUTELY EVERYTHING... AND YOU WANT TO GO HOME....

Symptoms   You were *so* desperate to emigrate. It has been number one on your 'to do' list since you can remember.

---

† With the help of an airplane/boat/train.

You've been in YNC for over 12 months[‡] and tried every trick in the book (and a few others), but it just isn't working and you think you want to go back home. And you feel totally overwhelmed by the prospect.

Cure　OK, this is a biggie. First of all, you need to release the pressure valve in your brain which is probably about to pop. There will be two Trains of Thought currently whizzing around your head.

The Practical Train is stressing out about the reality of the situation. The cost, the organisation required to get you back to Blighty, the thought of repacking your belongings, finding a new home, new job, and so on. Then there is **The Emotional Train** which, depending on what type of a person you are, could be completely freaking out. Worrying about what everyone will think about you 'giving up'[§] and beating yourself up about why on earth you decided to emigrate in the first place.

What you need to do first is focus on the Emotional Train and start getting your head around the prospect of returning 'home'. For while I am obviously a big advocate of emigration, I am an even bigger one of being happy.

Deciding that YNC isn't for you is a *positive* decision. Even though it might not feel like it. Yes, it might be complicated getting home but in years

---

[‡]　If you haven't given yourself 12 months to settle in...you haven't given yourself long enough...

[§]　Your words, *not* mine! Never view returning home as giving up.

to come, you won't regret trying. Honest! At least you were brave enough to find out for yourself and you now know for sure. We've all heard the saying 'life is a journey, not a destination', so your journey appears to have become a little more, well...convoluted, that's all.

But before you head for the departure lounge, I'll let you into a little secret...

A lot of people move abroad.

Then decide they don't like it and move back to the UK.

THEN decide they like the UK even less, and realise that 'abroad' actually wasn't that bad...and move back again!

Researchers are beginning to learn that the movement of people from one country to another doesn't just occur in an 'A to B' kind of fashion. There are all sorts of patterns that are constantly evolving where emigration can involve moving from one place to another, numerous times. Or it can be a cyclical movement with people returning to the Motherland and then heading off again. There are all sorts of configurations.

Whatever route or pattern you decide to embark upon, trust your decisions and do it confidently, because there really is no right or wrong when it comes to deciding what country you want to live in! The grass is *always* greener when peering over the Emigration Fence and you don't know how brilliant YNC really is until you have a chance to miss it (and that also goes for dear old Blighty!).

Whatever the outcome, the most important thing is to try to keep your options open and never close the Emigration Door behind you – whichever direction you're travelling in.

'FABULOUSNESS' WITHDRAWAL

Symptoms   You will only suffer from FAB withdrawal if you were the kind of Sensible Girl who was always out partying, drinking, socialising and generally being FABULOUS back home. Upon arrival in YNH you may suffer the odd dizzy spell or queasy turn at the prospect of having left all that Fabulousness behind.

This must not be mistaken for homesickness or GB sickness. Once you understand this, you are already on the road to recovery.

Cure   The way to ease FAB withdrawal is not to jump on the first flight home and hit the town with your old friends. That's just a quick fix and doesn't really solve anything.

What you need to do is find the fabulous places and people in YNH and party with them instead. Admittedly, if you have moved from West London to a small fishing village in Tunisia, you will have to dig a little deeper. But dig you must, as there will always be some kind of social event for a resourceful Sensible Girl to attend. Even if it is the Annual Lobster & Squid Dinner & Dance, you'll still have an opportunity to party!

HAIR LOSS

Symptoms So you didn't do your research properly. You needed a trim and you panicked. You took a chance on a shifty looking hairdresser whose roots were the same colour as her moustache...and you are now suffering the grim, grim consequences of her overly zealous feathering technique. OH, THE HORROR!

Suicidal feelings creep into your brain every time you catch a glimpse of yourself in the mirror. The very thought of going out in public, looking like a cross between Cher and Forrest Gump makes you want to vom. It's a world champion catastrophe.

Cure Buy a stylish hat...and never EVER return to that evil hair butcher again.

CHAPTER 22

YOUR EMIGRATION DE-BRIEF

Beginning is easy...continuing is hard.
JAPANESE PROVERB

Now that you're an expert on all things to do with your emigration, we should probably have a quick recap of how you've coped with the whole experience (and how you're likely to cope over the following months and years): a Sensible de-brief. What has the emigration process been like for you? More importantly, how DO you feel right now?

happy	☐	sad	☐	nervous	☐
depressed	☐	excited	☐	proud	☐
stupid	☐	scared	☐	fabulous	☐
hung-over	☐	anxious	☐	fat	☐
out of control	☐	bored	☐	inspired	☐
sic	☐	sick	☐	sick of trying	☐
afraid	☐	foreign	☐	smug	☐
clever	☐	confident	☐	stunningly beautiful	☐
lonely	☐	groovy	☐	energised	☐
hungry	☐	homesick	☐	misunderstood	☐
invincible	☐	depressed	☐	cross	☐
like a lie down	☐	like a man	☐	like a twat	☐
hysterical	☐	delirious	☐	miserable	☐
brave	☐	inebriated	☐	content	☐
exhausted	☐	unusual	☐	wonderful	☐
stunned	☐	hot and sticky	☐	agitated	☐
psychotic	☐	discombobulated	☐	sensible	☐

MOT SENSIBLE SCORE:

0–5	You big fat liar – re-count.
5–20	That's better, but I still want a bit more emotion.
20–51	Bingo!

As you know only too well, emigration is an emotional rollercoaster. It's going to be sunbeams and rainbows one minute and black clouds the next. You are going to wake up some mornings and feel like you could rule the world and then go to bed feeling like you can't even buy a packet of tampons without getting things wrong. But that's life and to be honest you can't always blame it on YNH either! You had crappy days back in the UK and you're going to have them here too. So don't fall into the habit of blaming everything that goes wrong on 'this stupid foreign country' you're now living in.

There is an invisible join where your emigration will become normal life again. You will not be the New Girl forever. It will probably take more than a year – but it might not. The thing with invisible joins is you don't know where they are!

A Sensible Girl called Anita[1] who successfully emigrated to Dubai (with a reformed Reluctant Partner, I might add) sums up what this whole book boils down to:

'The best bit of advice I got was from my dad. He said, "go and see what it's like. If you don't enjoy it or you can't settle, come home. No one will think any less of you. In fact, they will think more of you for trying and being honest with yourself, we will always be here for you." My dad really filled me with confidence and support by saying that.'

And that's all this book has tried to give you: confidence and support. You don't need anything else, because you've done the hard part. All you need to do now is enjoy your new life!

I want you to do one final experiment before you go.

I want you to look at the following pictures and select the one that most closely represents how you feel.

A)

B)

C)

A) Haven't you left yet? What are you waiting for – just do it!

B) Bravo – you did it!

C) ...yes...you really must learn to pay attention! Someone emigrates from the UK every three minutes.[2] And you, so it seems, WERE one of them!

Here's to you.

Here's to turning Your New Country into Your New Home.

You have successfully, and rather fabulously I might add, emigrated elegantly!

Cheers!

THE END BIT

...HAPPILY EVER AFTER?

It was 7.30 in the morning on a grotty Tuesday in the Borough of West Londinium.

The princess was staring out of the steamy Piccadilly Line carriage window, idly watching a couple of schoolboys throwing Wotsits at a pigeon when she was suddenly shaken out of her stupor by a beeping from her mobile phone.

GIDDAY STRANGER
HOWS LIFFE ON THE
OTHER SIDE OF
PLANET? ANY
UPDATE ON
YR LITERARY
MASTERPIECE?
WISH U WERE
COMING BACK
SOON LOVE MEGAN
XX

Attempting to cook up a witty response for her antipodean friend, the princess was rudely interrupted by a man the size of a pregnant walrus stepping deftly onto her newly purchased Chloé sandals.

'Is this seat taken love?' he snuffled.

She shook her head and went back to the text message.

The princess had worked with Megan in the publicity department of the Kingdom of Perth's Arts Festival for nearly a year before she left and came back to the UK. She had loved working there, had met some great people, made some good contacts and jammed her foot firmly in the 'Western Australian career door'. In fact she wished she was back there now and sent a text to her friend saying so.

Suddenly there was a loud yelp as a business woman got stuck in the train's closing doors. After a few moments of wrestling with her handbag, which was on the wrong side of the door and looked intent on staying that way, the doors re-opened and a grumpy-sounding driver requested that everyone 'stand clear'. The train sped on. The princess looked at her watch and realized she was late.

Not good.

She tried focusing on a row of shops that were whizzing past the window and wondered what the magical shopkeeper was up to back in the Western realm of the Great Red Continent. Since the princess had taken the job at the Arts Festival, she'd overheard that the magical shopkeeper and her vast bosom had married a billionaire and opened an emporium in the richest part of town. They had lost touch since the princess had moved. She made a mental note to text her, when she was a little more settled.

The train lurched violently and stopped in its tracks.

She stared at her own reflection and wondered whether a layered bob might suit her. Then she adjusted her vision to notice that it had started raining. Trying to ignore the fact that she was wearing highly inappropriate footwear (as usual), she wondered what the weather was like in the Kingdom of Perth.

It would be very shiny and blue, that's for sure...

Not grey.

The train didn't move, so the princess pulled the newspaper she had been sitting on, out from under her and started to flick through the dog-eared pages.

'POPULATION GETS LARGER – LONDON FULL OF FATTIES'

The princess casually tilted the not-so-subtle headline towards Mr Pregnant Walrus and raised her eyebrow, but he was too busy examining something he'd just extricated from his ear to notice.

The princess felt flustered. The city was doing her head in and an overwhelming feeling of claustrophobia began to wrap itself tightly around her throat. She hurriedly opened the vent above her head in the vain hope that a particle of fresh air, lost amidst the city's pollution, might just waft its way in and ease her panic attack.

A bald bloke next to her made an odd growling noise in his throat – reached over her and carefully slammed the vent shut again.

The princess sulked.

Nobody noticed.

The train made an unpleasant grating noise, juddered for ten seconds and then fell silent again. No one moved and neither did the train. Then a loud voice came on over the intercom:

'Londinium Transport would like to apologise for the delay, which is due to a fierce dragon that has escaped from the fiery bowels of the metropolis and crawled down onto the rails at Hounslow East...'

The carriage drew a collective breath and looked at each other with wide, excited eyes.

'...Nahh only jesting wiv ya,' laughed the comedy-genius-driver.[*]

'Some idiot's frown himself on the tracks so we're waiting for 'em to scrape 'im off, 'innit.'

Everyone including the princess looked a tad disappointed and went back to ignoring each other and the rather tragic information they had just been given.

Princess Sally wondered what Lord Grenville was doing. It would be mid-afternoon in the Kingdom of Perth. He would probably be driving from his office to the ocean in their old campervan and trying to find a parking spot by the beach. He had started surfing lessons just before she left him, and she imagined him dashing across the warm sand in search of some decent wave action.

---

[*]   Aren't they all?

The bald bloke opposite sneezed, something landed on the princess's skirt and the train lurched forward.

The princess felt sad. She missed Lord Grenville terribly. Just thinking about him made her wonder what she was doing here without him. Her little heart fluttered as she remembered their tearful goodbye, and she wished that he was sitting beside her now.

Stations rattled by and the princess wiped the condensation off the window to see damp tower blocks flashing past. She marvelled at how many people were crammed into these tiny living spaces – how they were all stacked up, one on top of the other, living like sardines and yet not even knowing what their neighbours looked like.

The princess thought about her enchanted cottage and wondered what her old neighbours, the lovely Mr & Mrs Galah, would be doing – aside from drinking beer and cooking sausages on their outdoor cooking fire.

Mr & Mrs G had become good friends over the last few years. The princess thought back to when they had first moved in to the neighborhood, worrying that she would never make any friends. But she had made a great many and now she'd left them all behind to sit on crappy Londinium Transport with the cast of Fraggle Rock for company.

A small, rather ugly looking child sitting further down the carriage began to scream. The princess glared at him while his oblivious mother studiously read an advertisement above the window for pregnancy tests.

The train doors closed once more and the princess realised that her stop was next. So she shoved the dog-eared newspaper down the back of her seat, bid a silent but emotional farewell to Mr Pregnant Walrus and gathered her bags. The train rattled down the tunnel and slowly pulled into her station, where it stood for about 20 seconds, before the driver noticed he'd forgotten to open the doors...

And then she was free, but she was also very late!

So she did that special 'running walk' that only commuters can do and made for the exit. And after a small altercation with a ticket machine, which stubbornly refused to accept her Oyster card, the princess dashed headlong into the crowds.

Twenty-five minutes later, Princess Sally finally found herself at the front of the queue and excitedly stepped forward. She had been waiting for this moment for a long time.

'Would you like a window or aisle seat, madam?' asked the lady behind the check-in desk at Ye Throwe Airport.

'A window seat, please,' said the princess 'and I don't suppose it could be nearer the front of the plane could it, I'm such a nervous flyer.'

The attendant gave a friendly smile and began tapping away on her computer.

'Righto, that's a window seat in business class,' winked the attendant, 'boarding from Gate 2393, to the Kingdom of Perth, your luggage will be automatically transferred straight through... enjoy your holiday, Mrs Grenville.'

'Oh thank you, but I'm not going on holiday,' beamed the princess. 'I've just finished my holiday and now I'm going home.'

And off she went on her way back to her Great Red Continent, her enchanted cottage and her beloved husband, Lord Grenville,

and she decided then and there, at the departure desk in Ye Throwe airport, that she was going to live happily ever after...
...and she is.

THE END

ACKNOWLEDGEMENTS

Thank you to everyone who so kindly helped me with this book...

My wonderful friends Nicki and Erica for patiently reading through the early stuff.

All the Sensible Girls dotted around the globe who contributed to this book: Anita, Jo, Karen, Miranda, Sheilagh, Shirley, Suzi, Tricia and everyone else I had the pleasure of talking to. It was the random conversations with friendly strangers that inspired me the most, so please forgive me for not remembering all of your names.

Lisa Palmer (counselling psychologist), Nynke Bruinsma and Sabina Eijkman (expat, life and career coaches (**www.theexpatcoaches.com**) and Lesley Sumner (qualified life coach...and sister-in-law!) – my wonderful panel of Emigration Experts.

The helpful people at the Office for National Statistics, in particular Geoff Wheeler and Jo Zumpe.

Mark Chapman, series producer of numerous *A Place In*...series at Tiger Aspect, Paul Beasley, editor of the super informative *Emigrate* ↗ Magazine (**www.emigrate2.co.uk**) and Oonagh Brennan (fashion director of *Company* magazine and my dear friend). Lizzy McNaney-Juster, Nicky Standley, Matthew Sanders.

Lorella Belli and Lisa Carden for believing in Elegant Escapology.

Lindy, Brian and Christopher, the Parkwood Posse; Alison Henley; and Mr & Mrs Galah (otherwise known as Megan and

Paul). All my lovely friends who didn't become disappearing acts. My 95-year-old grandma for telling me to 'go for it' and my mum and dad for letting their only child bugger-off halfway around the world.

But most of all, thank you to my wonderful husband who has been by my side through the whole adventure...you are my sunshine.

NOTES

PREFACE

1 *The Oxford Paperback Dictionary.* Oxford: Oxford University Press, 1994.

CHAPTER I

1 Jarski, Rosemarie. *The Funniest Thing You Never Said.* London: Ebury Press, 2004.

2 Emigration survey prepared on behalf of the BBC by ICM Research 2006.

3 Kuper, Simon. 'Moving Experiences'. London: *House and Home* section, *The Financial Times,* 31 January 2009.

4 Sriskandarajah, Dhananjayan, and Catherine Drew. *Brits Abroad: Mapping the Scale and Nature of British Emigration.* London: IPPR, 11 December 2006 (p.viii).

5 More than a year.

6 Original interview (via e-mail – July 2007). Nynke Bruinsma and Sabina Eijkman, life and career coaches from The Expat Coaches (**www.theexpatcoaches.com**).

7 Original interview (via e-mail - September 2007). Mark Chapman, series producer at Tiger Aspect.

8 Original interview with Lisa Palmer, Counselling Psychologist (via e-mail – July 2007).

9 Sriskandarajah, Dhananjayan, and Catherine Drew. *Brits Abroad: Mapping the Scale and Nature of British Emigration.* London: IPPR, 11 December 2006 (p. 93). (NB: this figure includes tourists.)

10 'Latvia benefits from boom in air travel'. *The Weekly Telegraph.* 23 April 2009 (p.16). (Stats taken from ONS 'Social Trends' report.)

11 Sriskandarajah, Dhananjayan, and Catherine Drew. *Brits Abroad: Mapping the Scale and Nature of British Emigration.* London: IPPR, 11 December 2006.

12 Sriskandarajah, Dhananjayan, and Catherine Drew. *Brits Abroad: Mapping the Scale and Nature of British Emigration.* London: IPPR, 11 December 2006 (p. 67).

13 Original interview, Lesley Sumner (via e-mail – 2007).

14 *Emigrate* ↗ Magazine issue 10 (pages 5 &10).
15 *Emigrate* ↗ Magazine issue 10 (p. 10).

CHAPTER 2

1 Price, Steven D. *The Best Advice Ever Given.* Connecticut: The Lyons Press, 2006.
2 Original interview (via e-mail – July 2007), Nynke Bruinsma and Sabina Eijkman, life and career coaches from The Expat Coaches (**www.theexpatcoaches.com**).
3 ONS news release on 'Population and Migration'. 15 November 2007 (p. 4).
4 Malewski, Margaret. *GenXpat: The Young Professional's Guide to Making a Successful Life Abroad.* Boston: Intercultural Press, 2005 (p. 33).
5 Frith, Maxine. 'The Big Question: How many Britons live abroad, and why do they leave home?' London: *The Independent*, 12 December 2006. (Based on IPPR research.)
6 Original interview (via e-mail – July 2007), Nynke Bruinsma and Sabina Eijkman, life and career coaches from The Expat Coaches (**www.theexpatcoaches.com**).
7 Sriskandarajah, Dhananjayan, and Catherine Drew. *Brits Abroad: Mapping the scale and nature of British emigration.* London: IPPR, 11 December 2006 (p. 70).

CHAPTER 3

1 Original interview (via e-mail – July 2007), Nynke Bruinsma and Sabina Eijkman, life and career coaches from The Expat Coaches (**www.theexpatcoaches.com**).
2 Original interview, Lesley Sumner (via e-mail – 2007).
3 The GROW model was originated by coach Graham Alexander (see **www.alexandercorporation.com**).
4 Sriskandarajah, Dhananjayan, and Catherine Drew. *Brits Abroad: Mapping the Scale and Nature of British Emigration.* London: IPPR, 11 December 2006 (p. 78).
5 Reproduced by permission of the Office for National Statistics (ONS): International migration estimates from IPS, 2003–2007), received 19 January 2009. 'Top Ten Countries of next residence for British citizenship by sex'.

CHAPTER 4

1 Price, Steven D. *The Best Advice Ever Given*. Connecticut: The Lyons Press, 2006.
2 Sriskandarajah, Dhananjayan, and Catherine Drew. *Brits Abroad: Mapping the Scale and Nature of British Emigration*. London: IPPR, 11 December 2006 (p. 20).
3 Sriskandarajah, Dhananjayan, and Catherine Drew. *Brits Abroad: Mapping the Scale and Nature of British Emigration*. London: IPPR, 11 December 2006 (p. 40).
4 Sriskandarajah, Dhananjayan, and Catherine Drew. *Brits Abroad: Mapping the Scale and Nature of British Emigration*. London: IPPR, 11 December 2006.

CHAPTER 5

1 Jarski, Rosemarie. *The Funniest Thing You Never Said*. London: Ebury Press, 2004.
2 Original interview (via e-mail - September 2007), Mark Chapman, series producer at Tiger Aspect.
3 Original interview (via e-mail – July 2007), Nynke Bruinsma and Sabina Eijkman, life and career coaches from The Expat Coaches (**www.theexpatcoaches.com**).
4 Original interview (via e-mail – July 2007), Nynke Bruinsma and Sabina Eijkman, life and career coaches from The Expat Coaches (**www.theexpatcoaches.com**).

CHAPTER 6

1 Jarski, Rosemarie. *The Funniest Thing You Never Said*. London: Ebury Press, 2004.
2 http://europa.eu/abc/european_countries/candidate_countries/index_en.htm
3 www.direct.gov.uk/en/BritonsLivingAbroad (Preparing to move or retire)
4 www.oecd.org/document/39/0,3343,en_2649_33931_43195111_1_1_1_37415,00.html, OECD website, International Migration Policies, "Keep Doors open to migrant workers" 30 June 2009.
5 www.immi.gov.au
6 Ministerial Statement by Senator Chris Evans Minister for Immigration & Citizenship – Changes to the 2008-09 Skilled Migration Program.

7 Information based on original interview with Daniel Bell, Regional Outreach Officer, WA.
8 Information based on original interview with Daniel Bell, Regional Outreach Officer, WA.
9 Longitudinal Immigration Survey: New Zealand (LisNZ). This survey is on-going where the LisNZ interviews the same migrants (approx 7,000) at six, 18 and 36 months on various immigration issues.
10 Or Irish Republic.
11 www.Telegraph.co.uk, British Expats 'forced from New Zealand'.
12 http://www.visabureau.com/newzealand/emigrate-to-new-zealand.aspx
13 http://www.immigration.govt.nz/migrant/general/generalinformation/news/ialaeffective.htm
14 www.Telegraph.co.uk, British Expats 'forced from New Zealand'.
15 The Longitudinal Immigration Survey: New Zealand (LisNZ) – Fast Facts 10.
16 http://www.usnews.com/articles/opinion/2008/12/31/us-population-2009-305-million-and-counting.html US News, Dec 2008 (original source US Census Bureau)
17 www.About.com (Immigration), "President Obama Launches Immigration Reform", by Jennifer McFadyen.
18 *Emigrate* ↗ Magazine August 09. How to Hustle for an H-1B (by Donna Scarlattelli).
19 http://www.cic.gc.ca/english/department/index.asp (Under Heading Immigration)
20 *Emigrate* ↗ Magazine 2008. Canadian Paperwork.
21 www.cic.gc.ca, Skilled workers and professionals who can apply 21 July 2009.
22 www.canadavisa.com/federal-skilled-worker-requirements-may-soon-change.html
23 www.canada.embassyhomepage.com
24 Emigrate ↗ Magazine. August 2009. 'Final Word' by David McKinney. Police Clearance Form article
25 www.uscis.gov

CHAPTER 7

1 Jarski, Rosemarie. *The Funniest Thing You Never Said*. London: Ebury Press, 2004.

2 Original interview with Lizzy McNaney-Juster, Brits Finance in USA (via e-mail – August 2007).
3 Malewski, Margaret. *GenXpat: The Young Professional's Guide to Making a Successful Life Abroad*. Boston: Intercultural Press, 2005.
4 Original interview with Shirley Pine (May 2006).

CHAPTER 8

1 www.quotedb.com
2 www.hmrc.gov.uk/cnr/p85_p85s.htm
3 www.hmrc.gov.uk/tdsi/overseas.htm
4 www.hmrc.gov.uk/cnr/app_dtt.htm
5 www.hmrc.gov.uk/cnr/nr_landlords.htm
6 www.hmrc.gov.uk/cnr/osc.htm#5
7 *Migrant Money* (magazine supplement to *Emigrate* ↗ Magazine). February 2009. 'Moving Your Assets' (p.10).
8 Someone who is fully regulated both in the UK *and* YNC. Try www.unbiased.co.uk as a start.
9 www.direct.gov.uk/en/Motoring/DriverLicensing/DG_10023103
10 www.rac.co.uk/know-how/going-on-a-journey/driving-abroad/countries-needed.cgi and www.theaa.com/getaway/idp
11 www.direct.gov.uk/en/Motoring/BuyingAndSellingAVehicle/ImportingAndExportingAVehicle/DG_4022582
12 www.direct.gov.uk/en/TravelAndTransport/TravellingAbroad/BeforeYouTravel/DG_4000019
13 A pet may not enter/re-enter the UK under the scheme until six calendar months have passed from the date that the blood sample was taken that gave a satisfactory result.
14 Original interview with Alison Henley, May 2006.
15 Original interview with Oonagh Brennan, August 2007.

CHAPTER 9

1 Jarski, Rosemarie. *The Funniest Thing You Never Said*. London: Ebury Press, 2004.
2 ICM survey prepared on behalf of the BBC (July 2006).
3 Original interview (via e-mail – July 2007), Nynke Bruinsma and Sabina Eijkman, life and career coaches from The Expat Coaches (**www.theexpatcoaches.com**).

4 Original interview with Lisa Palmer, Counselling Psychologist (via e-mail – July 2007).
5 Original interview with Lisa Palmer, Counselling Psychologist (via e-mail – July 2007).
6 Malewski, Margaret. *GenXpat: The Young Professional's Guide to Making a Successful Life Abroad.* Boston: Intercultural Press, 2005.

CHAPTER 10

1 Jarski, Rosemarie. *The Funniest Thing You Never Said.* London: Ebury Press, 2004.
2 Figures are based on either British Airways flight times or World Travel Guide website (**www.worldtravelguide.net/country/290/ international_travel/Middle-East/United-Arab-Emirates.html**).

CHAPTER 11

1 www.quotedb.com

CHAPTER 12

1 Original interview with Lisa Palmer, Counselling Psychologist (via e-mail – July 2007).
2 Original interview with Lesley Sumner (via e-mail – 2007).
3 Original interview with Lisa Palmer, Counselling Psychologist (via e-mail – July 2007).

CHAPTER 14

1 Price, Steven D. *The Best Advice Ever Given.* Connecticut: The Lyons Press, 2006.
2 Original interview with Oonagh Brennan, August 2007.
3 www.britishairways.com/travel/lcnews/public/en_nz
4 www.britishairways.com/travel/bagchk/public/en_gb
5 www.britishairways.com/travel/bagchk/public/en_gb

CHAPTER 15

1 Jarski, Rosemarie. *The Funniest Thing You Never Said.* London: Ebury Press, 2004.

CHAPTER 16

1 Jarski, Rosemarie. *The Funniest Thing You Never Said*. London: Ebury Press, 2004.

THE MIDDLE BIT

1 Jarski, Rosemarie. *The Funniest Thing You Never Said*. London: Ebury Press, 2004.

THE SENSIBLE GIRL'S IN-FLIGHT QUIZ

1 *Emigrate* ↗ Magazine. August 2009. "NZ Tops Expat Poll" (based on Natwest International Personal Banking (IPB) survey).

CHAPTER 17

1 Original interview (via e-mail – July 2007), Nynke Bruinsma and Sabina Eijkman, life and career coaches from The Expat Coaches (**www.theexpatcoaches.com**).

CHAPTER 18

1 Knorr, Rosanne. *The Grown-Up's Guide to Running Away from Home*. 2nd ed. New York: Ten Speed Press, 2008.
2 'All That's Best About Britain'. *The Independent*. 9 July 2007 + Wikipedia website: continuation of above article (**wikipedia.org/wiki/BBC_World_Service**).
3 Malewski, Margaret. *GenXpat: The Young Professional's Guide to Making a Successful Life Abroad*. Boston: Intercultural Press, 2005.
4 IPPR Sriskandarajah, Dhananjayan, and Catherine Drew. *Brits Abroad: Mapping the scale and nature of British emigration*. London: IPPR, 11 December 2006 (p. 46).
5 Malewski, Margaret. *GenXpat: The Young Professional's Guide to Making a Successful Life Abroad*. Boston: Intercultural Press, 2005.

CHAPTER 19

1 www.quotesandpoem.com
2 ICM Research on behalf of the BBC, July 2006.
3 IPPR Sriskandarajah, Dhananjayan, and Catherine Drew. *Brits Abroad: Mapping the scale and nature of British emigration*. London: IPPR, 11 December 2006 (ONS 2006a) – page 64
4 Original interview with Lisa Palmer, Counselling Psychologist (via e-mail – July 2007).
5 Bridges, William. *Transitions: Making Sense of Life's Changes*. 25th anniversary ed. New York: Perseus Books, 2004.
6 Original interview with Lisa Palmer, Counselling Psychologist (via e-mail – July 2007).
7 Kuper, Simon. 'Moving Experiences'. *FT Weekend*, House & Home, 30 January 2009.
8 Original interview with Lesley Sumner (via e-mail – 2007).
9 Original interview (via e-mail – July 2007), Nynke Bruinsma and Sabina Eijkman, life and career coaches from The Expat Coaches (**www.theexpatcoaches.com**).
10 Original interview, Lesley Sumner (via e-mail – 2007).
11 www.Expatwomen.com, quote taken from July 2007 Press Release / Andrea Martins
12 Original interview with Lisa Palmer, Counselling Psychologist (via e-mail – July 2007).
13 www.Expatwomen.com, quote taken form July 2007 Press Release, Robin Pascoe
14 Malewski, Margaret. *GenXpat: The Young Professional's Guide to Making a Successful Life Abroad*. Boston: Intercultural Press, 2005
15 Original interview (via e-mail – July 2007), Nynke Bruinsma and Sabina Eijkman, life and career coaches from The Expat Coaches (**www.theexpatcoaches.com**).
16 Woodward, Kath. *Understanding Identity*. London: Hodder, 2003.
17 Original interview with Lisa Palmer, Counselling Psychologist (via e-mail – July 2007).
18 Original interview with Lisa Palmer, Counselling Psychologist (via e-mail – July 2007).
19 *Emigrate ↗* Magazine. August 2009. "NZ Tops Expat Poll" (based on Natwest International Personal Banking (IPB) survey).

20 Frith, Maxine. 'The Big Question: How many Britons live abroad, and why do they leave home?' London: *The Independent*, 12 December 2006. (Based on IPPR research.)
21 Malewski, Margaret. *GenXpat: The Young Professional's Guide to Making a Successful Life Abroad*. Boston: Intercultural Press, 2005.
22 Original interview Erica Warren (May 2006).

CHAPTER 20

1 Original interview, Joanne Brabin (May 2006).

CHAPTER 21

1 Jarski, Rosemarie. *The Funniest Thing You Never Said*. London: Ebury Press, 2004.
2 *Emigrate* ↗. August 2009. "NZ Tops Expat Poll" (based on Natwest International Personal Banking (IPB) survey).
3 Malewski, Margaret. *GenXpat: The Young Professional's Guide to Making a Successful Life Abroad*. Boston: Intercultural Press, 2005.
4 Original interview (via e-mail – July 2007), Nynke Bruinsma and Sabina Eijkman, life and career coaches from The Expat Coaches (**www.theexpatcoaches.com**).

CHAPTER 22

1 Original interview with Anita Foley, October 2006.
2 Johnston, Philip. 'Emigration soars as Britons desert UK'. Telegraph. co.uk, 19 April 2008.

INDEX

accent affectation 292–3
accommodation booking 163–4
address, change of 171–2
advertising your stuff 137–8
age 90
agoraphobia 278–9
ailments
    post-emigrating 281–98
    pre-emigrating 176–85
aims 39–47
airport
    arrival 225–7
    departure 201–5
    outfit 187–8
alcohol 197
arrival 225–7
Australia 78–80

backpackers 9–10, 49
bad habits 276–7
banking
    abroad 96
    tying up finances 111–12, 172
beauty regime 170, 278, 298
belongings *see* stuff
boredom 185
businesses, starting new 44–5, 89
buying a home 98–9

calendars 66
Canada 83–4
Canadian Federal Skilled Worker
    Applications 83

car boot sales 136
cars 125–7
change, stages of 258–9
charity shops 135
charity work 245
children
    considering 33–4
    settling in 246
climate 53, 59, 284–5
clothes 138–9
compromise 24–5
cost of living
    abroad 102–3
    in the UK 7
Critical Skills List (CSL) 79
culture 252–5
CVs 238–40

de-brief 299–302
delusional nutcases 50
Department for Environment Food
    and Rural Affairs (DEFRA)
    129
Department of Homeland Security
    (DHS) 82
Department of Immigration 75
departure 201–5
destinations
    books about 70, 173
    choosing 52–61
    fantastic four 78–84
    flight times from the UK 161
    researching 54–60

top ten 51, 161
Diversity Immigrant Visa
    Programme 88
Double Taxation (DT) Agreement
    114
doubts 13–14, 37
driving licence 125

emergency money 112–13
emotions 299–300
employment opportunities 53
environment 275
Europe 75–6
European Economic Area (EEA)
    75–6
exchange rate 116–18
excuses 37

fabulousness withdrawal 297
families
    leaving 148–56
    morbid relatives 181–2
    relocating to be with 19–20
fashion sense displacia 283–4
finances *see* money
flights, booking 158–60
Freecycle 138
friends
    being forgotten about by 289–90
    finding 94, 104–7
    keeping in touch with old 247–8
    leaving 148–56
    turning weird 182–3
    vanishing 290–1
fun 94, 107–8, 168
future planning 72, 93–108

GB sickness 282

General Skilled Migration (GSM)
    visa 78–9
goals 39–47
GROW model 40–5

hair loss 298
handbag clearout 174–5
hand luggage 192–5
healthcare
    considering 132–4
    costs 36
    insurance 162
Her Majesty's Customs and
    Revenue (HMRC) 114
HiFX 117
holiday deficiency disorder 291–2
home
    finding a 94, 96–9
    last two weeks at 166–7
    letting your house out 119–21,
        141
    selling your house 119–21
    tying up your property 118–22
    see also renting a home
homesickness 256–73
    acceptance 260–1
    asking for help 264–6
    Brits abroad 266–9
    communication 262–3
    cure for 281
    forever 269–71
    patience 269
    positivity 262
    preparation 260
    routine 271–3
    staying healthy 263–4
    wanting to come home 294–7
house prices 58

identification 192
Immediate Skill Shortage List
  (ISSL) 80
immigration agencies 87–8
in-flight quiz 214–24
insurance 162–3
International Driving Permit (IDP)
  125
Internet
  for planning 64–6
  for settling in 230

jobs
  finding 94, 99–104, 238–41
  last two weeks of work 166
  starting new 241–3
  tying up 123–4
job skills 44–5

language
  considering 42–3, 58
  dictionaries/phrase books 70
  learning a new 277
last supper 197–8
leaving loved ones 148–56
leaving party 154–6
life changes 6
locals 57
luggage 188, 199–200

marriage, getting married abroad
  22
media 249–50
men
  misplaced husband 286
  organising emigrating 62–3
  see also partners
mental barriers 8–9

Migration Occupations Demand
  List (MODL) 78–9
misplaced husband 286
mobile phones 173–4
money
  cost of emigrating 58
  current financial situation 43–4,
    58
  emergency 112–13
  finding the 94, 95–6
  house prices 58
  reasons for emigrating 5–6
  and reluctant partners 24
  settling in 232–4
  tying up your finances 111–18
morbid relatives 181–2
mothers 33–4
music 174

National Insurance (NI)
  contributions 115
National Occupational
  Classification List (NOCL) 83
New Zealand 80–1

office politics 241
Organisation of Economic
  Co-operation and
  Development (OECD) 77
overstayers 91

packing your belongings 144–6,
  186–95
paperwork 74–92
  Europe 75–6
  fantastic four countries 78–85
  immigration agencies 87–8
  last two weeks 167

options 88–9
partners 89–90
planning 94
rest of the world 77–85
settling in 231–2
timing 90–2
parallel universe syndrome (PUS)
    293–4
parties, leaving 154–6
partners
    being driven mad by 285–6
    emotional baggage 18–19
    foreign 31–2
    paperwork, emigrating with
        89–90
    perks 279–80
    reluctant 18–19, 23–7, 286
    supportive 21–2
passports 86, 174
past management 72, 109–47
patience 184, 269
pay 102–3
pensioners 35–6
perks 274–80
pets
    considering 128–32
    settling in 247
Pet Travel Scheme (PETS) 129–31
phone call charges 184
planning 62–73
    address books 67
    alcohol 69
    bilingual dictionary/phrase book
        70
    birthday books 67–8
    box file 68
    calculator 67
    calendars 66

country-specific book 70
current co-ordination 72
ear muffs 69
future 72, 93–108
lists 67
master plan 72–3
past management 72, 109–47
USB 68–9
using the Internet 64–6
police clearance forms 86
positivity 262, 274–80
present buying 175
proactivity 11
psychotic freak out 178–9

quality of life 6, 53
quarantine 129

realism 42–5, 56
reasons for emigrating 3–6
recce 55–60
relationships 17
    see also partners
relocation agencies 97–8
reluctance
    from girls 24–5
    from partners 18–19, 23–7
renting a home
    abroad 98–9
    letting your house out 119–21,
        141
    settling in 233–7
    in the UK 118–19
Repatriation Insurance 162–3
Retirement Pension Forecast 115
returning home
    after 12 months 294–7
    rates 53

salary 102–3
saving 95
schizophrenia 176–8
selfishness 277–8
seniors 35–6
sense of direction 288–9
sense of humour 288
settling in 228–55
shipping
  your belongings 141–4
  your car 126–7
shopping 169–70
single status 18–20
skills 44–5
social life
  finding friends 104–7
  last two weeks before leaving
    168–9
  planning 94
  settling in 243–8
spanneritis 180–1
spontaneity 53–4
sport 246
statistics 2, 9
status 16–37
storage of belongings 140–4
students 89
stuff
  leaving behind 195
  tying up your 134–47, 167–8

tailing spouses 27–8, 286
tax 113–15
timing 90–2, 95–6, 101
travel arrangements 157–64, 249
tweakers 48
tying up loose ends 109–47

UK
  cost of living in 7
  dissatisfaction with 282
United States 81–3
United States Citizenship and
    Immigration Services (USCIS)
    82

vintage clothing stores 136–7
visualisation 12, 14–15

wages 102–3
wants 39–47
wardrobe maintenance 138–9
websites 64–6, 85
wedding plans 22
'what ifs' 179–80
wildlife 251
wish list 39–47
women
  organising emigrating 62–3
  reluctant 24–5, 286
workmates 244